Financementor

# MENTALISM :

## HOW TO ANALYZE PEOPLE AND KNOW WHAT THEY SECRETLY WANTS

# Table of contents

———

# Summary

Have you ever wanted to be good at reading people? Do you often feel that analyzing people and knowing what they want is your ultimate superpower?

Well, if you do, you'll be surprised and happy to know that it's no superpower at all. It's very possible. That is down to Mentality.

This book provides a way to make your dream of knowing what people secretly want come true.

In this book, you will learn what it means to be a mentalist and the secret techniques that make them stand out. That's not all.

You will also learn about the various ways to read and understand the human body language perfectly. You will also understand what motivates people and how this can help you be a better mentalist.

Mentalism can seem intimidating when starting. We understand how frustrating it can be. This book presents you with all the tricks and skills you need to be a mentalist. You also get to know the various ways you can use those skills to make a nice income for yourself.

So, if this excites you, you are one purchase away from knowing everything you ever wanted to know about mentalism.

# Introduction

---

What if you could know what people were thinking? Just thinking about that question can set your imagination to go wild. However, you probably think that's all it is. An imagination that will never see the light of the day. You're wrong!

It is possible to know what someone is thinking. No, it definitely isn't magic! It's something more practical and can be learned. Mentalism!

For many people, thinking about mentalism might invoke some thoughts. Some people regard mentalism as a form of stunt. They view mentalism as something meant to be done only on stage. To others, mentalism involves simple tricks that can be explained. However, there is so much more to mentalism.

It can be the key to understanding things about people that you never thought were possible. It can be the way to knowing what people really want and the message they are passing. Would you like to do more? Would you like to be an expert at recognizing the signs people give? Would you love to become an expert in mind-reading? Well, that's exactly why I wrote this book.

## What You Will Get From Reading This Book

If this is the first time you are reading about mentalism and its awesome benefits, then this book is for you. It starts off by giving you a brief introduction to mentalism. We will also talk about why this mentalism is quite different from other related concepts such as hypnosis and telepathy. We will also be discussing some similarities between these concepts.

If you ever wondered how or if mentalism is tied in with psychology, then you are in luck. We will discuss these ties and their meanings if you want to learn about mentalism.

If you thought that mentalism was just for the stage show, then think again! This book will explain how mentalism is used in various industries and sectors. If you have decided to become a mentalist, there are some things you should know. You can find these things in chapter two of this book.

To know what people think, you have to understand them and their behavior. I totally agree with that statement. Most human gestures and emotional response tell you something important about them. This book shall cover some of the most important gestures and the hidden meaning behind them.

At the center of learning about mentalism and what people want is learning to read people. This book shall discuss this in great detail. You can expect to see some of the common behaviors of liars and other human gestures.

No matter how much we think we know humans, they often surprise us. This is because of the different personalities that exist in the world today. This book contains everything you need to know about various personalities and how they affect mentalism.

Wish you knew some mentalist tricks? If you do, then this book will bring joy to your heart. In chapter 9 of this book, we will discuss the various tricks that are popular today. We will also provide step-by-step instructions on how you can perform these things effortlessly.

Learning all these things can be really entertaining. However, if you want to be pro at mentalism, you need to know more. That's why we will also discuss some of the best ways you can keep improving at mentalism.

One thing is certain when you read this book. You are getting loads of value for your money. You are going to get incredibly better at reading people. Finally, you are going to develop the right skills needed to be a mentalist. We would talk all about that in the final chapter of this book.

## Why You Need This Book

Before you opened up this introduction, you probably have a knack for mind-reading. You probably think it's pretty cool. Because of this, you are willing to put in the work.

For many people, they start their journey by just looking through the internet and watching videos. They get tiny bits of what they are looking for here and there. While that might work a bit, it's bound to fail for some reasons.

First, learning about mentalism is so broad. Each article you see on the internet or video you watch will only give you a small part of what you need to know. Learning the process of mind reading and human behavior is also quite broad. You'll never get all the parts you need.

You are also going to have to sieve through accurate and inaccurate information. You might spend hours reading articles that are outdated or simply lies. This book allows you to get all the information you need in one place.

Furthermore, the information in the book has been tested and is accurate in all regards. It is one of the safest bets you can make through your journey to mentalism.

Here are some other benefits you can expect by the end of this book.

### You Learn Everything About Mentalism

While everyone talks about mentalism, you have to admit that it can be hard to learn its intricacies. This book is going to tell everything about mentalism and how and why it is beneficial today. It's something you should definitely not miss.

### Boost Your Self-Confidence

It's easy for things to go wrong with mentalism. You can make mistakes here and there. Suddenly, you don't feel so confident anymore. This book will help you boost your self-confidence. By learning about the skills you need, you'll know exactly what you need to do to achieve your targets.

### It Teaches You All You Need To Keep Improving

Even when you learn the basics and advanced things about mind-reading, it might be hard to keep moving in the right direction. I know that I found that difficult. However, with time, I found some really cool things that kept me going in the right direction.

I want to share these things with you. This book will help you to keep improving your skills.

## Why You Can Trust the Author

There are many reasons why you can trust me. However, I'd just give you one. I have been there! I have been in your shoes, wanting to learn all about mentalism. I know how frustrating it can be to not have the full information in your grasp.

That is one of my main reasons for writing this book. I want you to learn everything that made me great at reading people's minds. Because of my earlier struggles, I desperately want to see you succeed regardless of your goal or purpose in reading this book.

I can assure you that by the end of this book, you will be ready to take on the world.

## What Happens If You Do Not Buy This Book?

So here's the thing! You can choose not to buy this book. However, it might not be in your best interests. If you really want to become a pro at analyzing and reading people well, then you just need this book. Without it, you might never get some of the best pieces of advice from this book.

Also, you might never really become one of the best mentalists out there!

## It's Now Or Never

In the end, it's really now or never. If you choose to continue reading this book, you'll learn some amazing things in your life. If you choose not to read this book, you'll never know what was on the other side of trying it out.

If you have decided to read this book, then it's time to turn to chapter one.

# Chapter One - Introduction to Mentalism

————

## Introduction

Everything that ever existed on earth had a beginning. We both know the day we were born. It's often said that if you want to understand a concept or a person better, you have to go back to the beginning. I agree with that statement. It also applies to mentalism.

To understand what mentalism and the act of mind-reading is all about, we really have to go back to the start. This chapter will be exploring that in its entirety. There's more.

We will also be considering the uniqueness of mentalism and how it compares to other similar concepts. This chapter will also look at the ties that mentalism has to psychology and what this means for all mentalists.

If you want to be a mentalist, this is where you have to start. In this chapter, we will consider who really can be a mentalist.

If you are ready for our journey, let's start from the beginning.

## The Origin of Mentalism

The very first signs of mentalism are unknown. For many people. It can be traced way back to biblical times. This was a period where people considered to be oracles and seers existed. It's easy to see why this was rampant. The kings of those times believed strongly in divinity and other supernatural thinking.

It was not just the kings who believed in these abilities. People also held them in high regard. Most times, households would consult oracles before big decisions were made.

While this might have shown some real promise in regards to mentalism, it still could not be considered to be mentalism in its entirety.

The first real act of mentalism can be traced to the 1500s. Girolama Scotto was said to have been a pioneer of mentalism. He is famous for conducting the very first mentalist trick or act in 1572.

While this was the first sign, things would not kick-off for the next 300 years. When it did kick-off, mentalism would soared in popularity and take on a lot more importance. It has been rumored that most great men of the early 1900s relied on mentalists in making decisions.

A classic example of this claim is that of Hitler and Erik Jan Hanussen. It is this mentalist that told Hitler a lot about the impact of dramatic performances in public.

In our world today, there are still so many mentalists out there making a difference. This has been aided by the boom of the internet and other advancements. Now, you can search for the term on the internet and get a wide array of resources. It is because of these advancements that you can now read this book.

Some of the more contemporary popular mentalists include Colin Cloud, Peter Turner, and Max Junior.

## Mentalism and Psychics

While mentalism certainly has a rich culture, there is nothing about it that is related to fake tricks done by stuntmen. These types of people are usually called psychics or stage magicians. The world of mentalism is completely different from card tricks.

In recent times, mentalists have taken their time to actually debunk several so-called "mentalist tricks" done by these people. Examples of popular psychics include Tyler Henry and John Edwards.

While it is clear that these are two very different things, other concepts have a unique relationship with mentalism. While this may be true, they are all very different concepts.

We shall now consider at least two of these concepts by comparing them to mentalism. This will give us a good overview of what they are and their relationship with mentalism.

## Mentalism and Hypnosis

Hypnosis and mentalism are often interlinked by so many people. If you're not careful, you'll start to think that they are one and the same thing. However, they couldn't be more different.

Let's consider some of the differences between both concepts.

### 1. The Meaning of the Concepts

The first place to start would be the meaning of both concepts. Mentalism is the ability to read people and manipulate the mind. It stems from immense practice and experience.

Hypnosis, on the other hand, couldn't be more different.

Hypnosis is the act of putting an individual in a sleeplike state. Most times, the act of hypnosis is voluntary. It is often referred to as a state of trance. Others refer to it as a situation where the imaginations of the one hypnotized are at their highest level.

Regardless, from their definition, you can already see the differences emerging.

## 2. Their Aim

The aim of both concepts is largely different. For mentalism, it is often done to know and manipulate the minds of others. Mentalists sought to analyze and secretly know what another person is thinking. This is fundamentally different when placed side by side with hypnosis.

The aim of hypnosis is to help the patient to have more awareness over their preferences and behaviors. It also helps people to control their emotions as well as desires. Hypnosis has also been used several times to bring back memories that are important or have been suppressed due to traumatic events.

The aims of hypnosis can change depending on intentions. Sometimes, hypnosis can be used on stage for entertainment purposes.

## 3. How It Is Performed

For hypnosis, the usual method is to put the patient in a form of trance. The patient is kept in this state voluntarily. This state allows the patient to lower their inhibitions. It also makes them very responsive to directions given to them by others. This allows them to bring back whatever event or memory that might be the issue. It's also a good way to make jokes on stage.

For mentalism, the manner of execution is quite different. The participant is fully awake and their minds are fully active. Mentalism works with the aid of gestures and human movements. The mentalist can understand certain messages the body is emanating because of these signals.

## 4. Use of Both Concepts

Most concepts are used in various capacities. Hypnosis is used to treat people who are suffering from trauma. They can also be used on stage. Mentalism can affect a wide range of sectors (as we will see in future chapters).

# Are Hypnosis And Mentalism Similar In Any Way?

Since mentalism and hypnosis seem so different, are they similar in any way? Yes, they are! In fact, the very basis of both concepts is one and the same. Let's consider a few similarities.

They are both concerned about the mental world.

If there is one thing we can agree on, it is the fact that both concepts are focused on the brain. However, their methods or aims are completely different.

## The Same End-Goal

Regardless of how they are both executed, both concepts and practices have the same goal. They seek to control and influence the mental aspect of a participant. Mentalism does this to know what people think while hypnosis does it for completely different reasons.

# Mentalism and Telepathy

Telepathy is another concept that is definitely linked to mentalism. It's not hard to see why. Telepathy also involves thoughts, expressions, and emotions. However, how it influences these thoughts and expressions is completely different from mentalism.

If you are having a bit of a problem understanding the differences between mentalism and telepathy, these three main differences will help.

## 1. Their Meaning

Telepathy is all about expressing yourself without talking. That's not all. These thoughts and expressions are transmitted to someone else who just gets it. Telepathy, however, also involves thought reading and is often related to some forms of magic. Mentalism, on the other hand, could not be more different.

Mentalism involves manipulating the minds to believe what you want. But there's more. It is also the ability to read people and know what they secretly want. While this may sound similar to telepathy, it isn't. Mentalism makes use of human gestures and signals to understand the message being passed. Telepathy is performed without any physical interaction between the body senses.

That makes them completely different!

## 2. Execution

Telepathy does not involve any physical presence. It's simply a thing of the mind. It involves focusing your thoughts to send a message to others. Most people who claim to be telepaths will often practice yoga and spend long hours meditating. There is however no real study on telepathy and how reliable it is.

Mentalism, on the other hand, is more practical. It involves physical interaction between two people. It also makes use of the senses during its execution. Mentalism is also a form of social science. This makes it different from telepathy.

## 3. Its Use

Mentalism has found itself useful in several industries in the world today. In fact, there are several movies revolving around mentalism today. Telepathy, on the other hand, is more focused on tricks. Telepaths are often on stage performing tricks or telepathic skills.

## How Are These Two Concepts Connected?

Yes, telepathy and mentalism are very different. However, the one thing that does connect them is their relationship with the brain. Just like hypnosis, telepathy seeks to send messages to the brain without using normal means of communication. Mentalism, on the other hand, uses human gestures and emotions to understand what the brain is trying to pass along.

The history of telepathy and mentalism is also tied together. Washington Bishop was someone who both claimed to be telepathic and mentalist at the same time. While this is true, these two concepts could never be more different.

## Bottom Line

So here's the bottom line. Mentalism is clearly different from both hypnosis and telepathy. One of its main differences is its practical nature. This makes it reliable and easier to understand. Another reason why it's different is its clear ties to Psychology.

# The Ties between Mentalism and Psychology

When most people think about mentalism today, they hardly think about academics. Some might even have the wrong notion that mentalism is all about tricks and not real. They are wrong. That's not all. Mentalism has deep ties with psychology.

In previous centuries, the study of mentalism was deeply rooted in academia. Mentalism was often described as a human science. It was meant to explain the thoughts and emotions of humans to the world.

Mentalism was considered to be a sub-branch of philosophy. It was led by some really well-known philosophers like René Descartes and Immanuel Kant. Their aim for studying mentalism was to truly understand the thought process of humans through logic.

While this branch probably started with excitement, it failed to achieve what these great men were looking for. This was probably due to the limits which were placed on psychological analysis then. Anecdotes and dissections were the most used experiments during this period. These will eventually form what we now know as psychology.

In time, other men such as William James would eventually carry out this branch of psychology. It is now known as mentalism psychology.

## What It Means For Mentalism

It's clear then that there was a huge link between psychology and mentalism. As time went on, more scientists started to adopt what is now known as behaviorism. Behaviorism focuses on the various human observations that can be seen and explained. One of the reasons for this change was the feeling that pure mentalism psychology was based on guesses and assumptions.

However, soon enough, other ways of knowing the various processes that occur in the brain became possible. Thus, behaviorism soon faded into cognitive psychology.

Mentalism in the modern day is a mixture of both the original mentalism psychology and behaviorism. This means that a mentalist would often attempt to understand the way the mind works through observation of certain human gestures.

While mentalism today is not a big part of psychology, it remains a key interest of this field to understand the neural activities that take place in the body.

So what does this mean? Does it mean that being a mentalist is reserved for people who are philosophers or scientists? Who can really be a mentalist?

## Can Anyone Become A Mentalist?

Well, the answer is yes. What does it take to become a mentalist? Despite how tricky it might seem, we all can become a mentalist if we want to. However, it's one thing to want to become a mentalist and another thing to actually become one.

To become a mentalism, you are going to need a lot of practice. Here are some things you should probably start practicing right now.

# 1. Quick and Accurate Judgements

The key to becoming a good mentalist is actually trusting your judgment. That really is the first step. If you cannot trust it, you can never be a mentalist. Most people today make quick judgments based on their emotions or how they are feeling. That's now how judgments made by a mentalist work.

Mentalists are often very observant. This means they can often spot some patterns that could have been easily missed by other people. If you want to see if you can turn your observant switch on, start by noticing smaller things you usually don't pay attention to. For example, if you greet someone, try to know the texture of their hands.

Another example of being observant is to notice the ring marks on the fingers. You can know if someone is married without even asking!

# 2. Know yourself first

Now, I know you are probably excited about trying out your observant skills on someone else. However, why not try it on yourself first. There are so many things you can learn by just looking in the memory.

For example, you have probably heard about how happy thoughts make the eyes dilate and bad thoughts make them constrict. Well, have you actually seen it happen before? Just practicing with yourself by looking in the mirror can give you a good idea of what to expect.

Another way you can observe yourself is to check what happens when you are angry, nervous, or jealous. How does your body respond to this feeling? Does your breathing pattern change? You can pretty do this for every emotion that you feel.

# 3. The Art of Asking Questions

If there is something that is in the realm of mentalism, it is the art of persuasion. To persuade someone, you have to learn how to ask questions. Not just any questions. Mentalists learn to be adept at asking leading questions. Asking questions is a good way to see how people react to certain things or knowledge.

The important thing about asking leading questions is that it allows the other person to express themselves. If there is one thing that calms people down, it is the feeling that they are being understood.

Leading questions are also very vague in nature. If you think that is a bad sign, then you definitely need to think again. Asking people vague questions will leave those gaps you want to learn more about. When people answer, they end up telling you much more than you asked for.

## 4. Observation Is Very Important

As earlier mentioned, being able to observe people is very important. However, you should also be able to observe the environment around you. To do this effectively, start by forming a habit of looking around any place or room you find yourself in. Having a look can quickly allow you to pick up the energy in the room.

For example, there are a dozen ways to know immediately when someone is nervous. Standing as close to the door as possible can mean nervousness. If someone in the room gives his body focused on someone else, it can show an interest in that person. They really don't have to use their eyes during this process. If everyone seems to seek one person's approval or opinion, then you probably have the top dog in your sight.

These little signs can tell you a lot. Being observant is the first thing to focus on if you want to become a mentalist.

## Learn How to Plant Ideas

Sometimes, reading someone's mind can be as easy as planting ideas in people's heads without their knowledge. For most mentalists, simply use a recurring word in an earlier discussion with the person. By doing so, they plant an idea deep into their subconscious.

For example, mentioning the word "dog" in a previous conversation will make the person think about dogs when asked to think of an animal.

Planting ideas in people's minds take time. To master this skill, you just have to practice. We'll talk more about improving your skills in the next few chapters of this book.

So can anyone be a mentalist? Yes, they can! However, they need to start making the things listed above a habit. It will really help them achieve their goal.

## Top Qualities of a Mentalist

The habits above will only get you so far. Mentalists also have certain qualities that make them stand out. Let me be honest with you. You can learn everything you need to know and more in this book. However, if you do not have these qualities listed below, it might be difficult to become a great mentalist.

Here are some of the top qualities that every mentalist has.

### 1. Passion

I'm just going to say it. Mentalism is not a walk in the park. Make one mistake and everything can go wrong. It's not something you should do if you don't have a passion for it. With mentalism, there is just so much you have to learn and keep learning.

When the workload becomes too much, it is the passion that will keep you going. So, embrace the passion. Start reading everything you can about mentalism starting from this book. Look out for all the essentials that you are going to need. Take the time to develop your own technique of mentalism.

With the right amount of passion, you will be unstoppable!

### 2. Confidence

Half of your job as a mentalist will be all but done if you can convince the other person you know exactly what you are doing. That is all down to how confident you are. So make sure you turn on the style. Most times, looking confident can be as easy as donning a smile or small smirk.

Just make sure that your nerves cannot be sensed by just looking at you. That really is the first step.

### 3. Observant

We have hardly gone past the first chapter of this book. Yet, being observant has been mentioned a lot of times. That is because it really is important. To some mentalists, it is actually one of the core things every mentalist should master.

The truth is if you are not observant, you cannot notice the little things or details that convey the message. So, take some time out to work on being observant enough. It really is the turning point for any mentalist.

### 4. Be Charismatic

Being a mentalist definitely means that you emit an aura of confidence and originality. To pull this off, you need high doses of charisma. People need to take a look at you and feel that you are someone that should be listened to. People need to believe that you are a mentalist.

If people feel that you are shaky and unsure of yourself, then you will see the effect you have on people disappear into thin air. Being charismatic also means that you are actually believable. In the world we live in, most people treat mentalist skills with doubts. This is partly due to ignorance about the entire practice.

However, with enough charisma, you should be able to convince them otherwise.

### 5. You Have To Be Unique

The truth is that there are a bunch of mentalist tricks out there. Some are more popular than others. Most people have heard of the smallest of tricks used by mentalists. So, doing the same tricks over and over again will make you look boring or repetitive.

So, strive to achieve a form of uniqueness. To be that unique in mentalism, you have to keep reading and learning new things. In the world of mentalism, being the best is really all that matters.

### 6. Mentalism Is Always Interesting

Finally, you have to keep things interesting. Mentalism is not boring. Most of the time, people are intrigued with mentalism because of the exciting feeling it brings. If you make your craft to be boring, then people will feel less inclined to listen to what you have to say. Worse, they might even start to doubt you know much about mentalism.

So here's the bottom line. You have to keep things moving in the right direction. You also have to develop the right habits and attitudes to succeed. Without that, you are never going to make the right progress.

## Conclusion

It is clear then that mentalism is simply a rich branch of psychology. It blends its understanding with pure individualistic skills superbly. The next few chapters will focus on honing your craft as well as other basic things you should know.

However, let us first talk about why mentalism is simply more than just a show. Turn the page to keep reading.

# Chapter Two - Importance of Mentalism

## Introduction

As we have seen in the first chapter, mentalism is simply more than trickery or stunts. It has its ties or roots deep into psychology. For some, it could even be the practice of psychology. To be a mentalist involves a lot of work and action. This is understandable. Mentalism is an art on its own. It requires immense dedication and practice. However, what's the point of it all?

You will be forgiven for asking this question. At first glance, it might be difficult to see the impact mentalism has on the world in general. Probably, all you think it does is make people look good on stage. That definitely will not appeal to anyone who wants to make an impact in life.

So this chapter is going to address these concerns. We are going to talk extensively about the importance of mentalism. But that's not all we are going to address.

We are going to talk about the various industries and places where mentalism can excel. Finally, I am going to walk you through some of the things you should prepare yourself for when you decide to learn mentalism.

So if you are ready for this incredible journey, let's begin!

# Why is Mentalism so important?

### 1. Self-Development

The first reason why mentalism is so important is self-development. Just think about it. When you learn or practice mentalism, you learn a whole bunch of skills. Mentalism is related to mental growth and awareness. With mentalism, you learn to be more observant, charismatic, and intellectual. That's not all.

Mentalism teaches you how to make conversation with people. Being a mentalist allows you to understand people and their gestures. When you put all this together, it's pretty clear that studying mentalism is simply perfect for self-development. You learn so many new things in one quick go.

### 2. Improves your Thinking Process

If there's one thing you are bound to learn from mentalism, it's improving your thought process. Here's why. Mentalism requires a lot of thinking and observation. To learn about human gestures, personalities, and what they mean takes time. Therefore, to enter a room and be able to tell who is who in that room is some skill.

That is all possible with mentalism. It keeps you thinking and analyzing various ideas. The thinking process also means it allows you to think outside of the box. This certainly adds to the creativity of an individual. That is the gift given by mentalism.

### 3. Mentalism Takes Your Communication to the Next Level

At the heart of it all, mentalism is really about communication. It's about communicating without having to say long complex sentences. In my view, mentalism is the fastest way to communicate with others.

Furthermore, all humans need to actively communicate with each other. This is the way we create connections and memories with each other. Without enough communication, there will be a lot of misunderstandings between people and even friends.

So, by learning mentalism, you now have that ability. You get the opportunity to understand people and their secret desires.

## 4. The Art of Persuasion

Persuasion in the world we live in today is a highly sought skill. Just think of all the marketing companies we have today and the influencers that come with them. These guys pay a lot of money to influence large audiences to buy a particular product.

While mentalism is definitely not meant for the marketing industry, it teaches people the art of persuasion. Mentalism focuses on understanding people's desires, fears, and motivations. It teaches them how to use these desires and fears to influence people positively. With the art of persuasion, you can have a great impact on the choices that others make.

## 5. It Provides a Source of Income

Finally, people can make a great career out of mentalism. The skills you learn as a mentalist are highly sought out in most places. Mentalism is so important because it creates a whole different industry. It all depends on what you want to use your mentalist skills to do.

However, you can be sure that mentalism can put food on the table.

Talking about industries, there are so many places today that you can definitely excel as a mentalist. This might go against popular beliefs that mentalists are simply for the show and entertainment. However, you could not be further away from the truth.

## Sectors where Mentalists Excel the Most

If you are thinking of becoming a mentalist, this question has surely been in your mind for some time. You probably were bothered about the career pattern of a mentalist and how you can make money from your talents.

To be honest, that's a legitimate concern and one that should be addressed. To remove this worry from your mind, we have gathered some of the best industries and places that we think a mentalist will fit in just fine.

## 1. Police

One of the obvious places that the mentalist will fit in perfectly is within the police force. Just think about it. There are so many criminals who are caught that are unwilling to talk or cooperate. Having a mentalist on the police force goes a long way in helping them understand the minds of a criminal.

While mentalists are not mind readers, they can often understand other people's behavior from their gestures, eye movements, and even small actions. This will be invaluable for the police force.

Mentalists will also be excellent detectives. They have some of the best techniques and methods for asking questions. Add to this their observant skills and you have someone who really knows what they are doing. A mentalist is a really perfect addition to a police force.

## 2. Entertainment Industry

When people hear about mentalists, this is often the first place or industry that comes into play. The entertainment however is a trickery place for mentalists. People often compare mentalists to fake magicians on stage. But, this is completely wrong.

Mentalists do not claim to be magicians. Instead, they use gestures and human interactions to accurately predict their actions.

### 3. Private Detectives

Mentalists can also be private detectives. While private detectives are often hired to dig into someone's past or try to understand their present, there is a lot of motives that have to be understood. The private detective is expected to understand what the person is doing to make sure that the investigation goes smoothly.

In many ways, this is perfect for mentalists. Mentalists are very observant people. This means that they will likely be able to understand what people are thinking and why they are behaving in a certain way just by watching them.

So as a mentalist, you can definitely become a private detective.

### 4. Freelancer

Mentalists can also freelance. In fact, the majority of mentalists are often in the gig economy. This is because it makes perfect sense. By doing this, mentalists can actually control the income that they make.

In the United States, it is estimated that mentalists make about $500 upwards to more than $2,000 for every gig they take and complete. That's a lot of money! Get a couple of gigs per month and you will no doubt be able to create a stable income for yourself.

### 5. Book Writer and Teacher

As a mentalist, there's one other area you probably have not thought about. You can teach other people the skills that you have taken so long to master. Once you have a bit of expertise, you can start a course about mentalism.

Another way you can teach people is by writing eBooks like the one you are reading now. You will be surprised at how much you will be able to make with mentalism.

It is clear then that being a mentalist does not mean you have to sacrifice having a progressive career. Being mentalist offers you all that and more. You can also have a more balanced work-life ratio if you choose when and how you decide to work as a mentalist.

So, if you have decided to become one or learn how to read people more accurately, you should definitely have a complete picture of what you are getting yourself into.

## What You Should Know When You Decide To Build A Career in Mentalism

### 1. It's A Gradual Process

Learning mentalism is not going to catapult into stardom in a week. You are not going to become a pro in a month. Mentalism is an entire discipline on its own. So, you have to realize that it is going to take time to get to where you want to be.

You are going to have to learn the skills needed and become better at them. If you really want to fasten the entire process, then you should take time to practice it every day.

### 2. You Are Going To Need a Good Foundation

Before you hop into the world of mentalists, you need to lay a proper foundation for yourself. If not, you will probably not go far. A proper foundation can be as easy as just making sure you learn the basics. You should also invest in your talents.

Buy books that talk about mentalism. Find ways to make sure you are always learning as much as you can about it. Watch videos about how to read people better. You'll be surprised at the impact this will have on you.

### 3. Exploit the Mentalist Community

Just like any other profession, being a mentalist means that you have other colleagues or professionals who have been in the business way longer than you. When you are starting out, reaching out to them can really be helpful.

You will learn so much from them. The best part about this is that they are not too difficult to find. As you hone your skills, you will also be able to help others do better.

### 4. It Won't Be All Smooth Sailing

Chances are that you just cannot wait to finish this chapter. Let's just get to the main course! However, you must know this. Learning mentalism is not all smooth sailing. Sometimes, you are going to get things completely wrong. This might be in public or during practice.

When this happens, you might feel embarrassed and struggle to get past it. So, prepare yourself mentally for this situation. If you are prepared and know that this is going to happen, you will be prepared to handle things better.

### 5. It Might Not Work Out

You also have to face a very sad possibility. Despite your best efforts to learn about the mentalist world, your efforts might not pay off. Things might just not work out. It might not even be your fault. You have to understand that happens. However, you cannot really know until you have tried.

When it doesn't work out, you have a choice to make. You can keep trying or just look for another path. I cannot tell you to keep trying forever to be a mentalist. Instead, I can tell you to choose the path that you feel will lead you closer to your dreams and ambitions.

## Conclusion

Mentalism is one hell of a ride, and I'm ready to show you everything I know about it. While mentalism is definitely broad, we will be paying close attention to analyzing people's thoughts and emotions. This means that we will consider most things that can allow you to do this.

In the coming chapters, we will discuss ways you can read people's gestures and what they mean. We will also discuss how people's personalities influence their decisions and their actions.

However, before we go into that, we are going to talk about something that is equally just as important. The art of cold reading.

# Chapter Three - The Art of Cold Reading

———

Can you get a complete picture of someone by just looking at the way they walk, their body language, or their hairstyle? Well, if you can't, that's okay. Not many people can actually. In fact, this is often referred to as an art. In most parts of the world, it is known as cold reading.

If you want to be a mentalist who can understand people's feelings and desires, this is really where your journey begins. You have to understand the various things that make people tick. Then, by cold reading people, you can present yourself in a truly stunning way.

If you find this exciting, then you are definitely on the right track. It is hands down one of the most interesting parts of being a mentalist. If you can manage this, then you are probably on your way to getting the most out of your career.

So, in this chapter, we will focus on the art of cold reading and what you can do to improve your cold reading techniques. The chapters that will come after this one will have elements of cold reading in them. This is because it is such a broad topic with many subtopics.

However, I will do my best to cover them really well.

## What Is The Art Of Cold Reading?

Simply put, cold reading is the art of making accurate guesses. However, these guesses are not just guesses. They are assumptions made

based on so many factors. These factors include the age of the participant, their educational qualifications, the way they speak, and what they
think about religious beliefs.

From these factors, a mentalist can then pick up on some important
signals. These signals can be analyzed to ensure that they are heading in
the right direction. If you master the cold reading, you will almost always
be accurate with your readings.

## Why Does The Cold Reading Method Work?

One of the reasons why the cold reading works is due to the Barnum
effect. Don't worry, we'll talk more about this effect in a later chapter.
However, this refers to when a description that fits so many people or in
fact everyone else seems to fit just right into it.

This thus makes participants believe that those personality descriptions must be specific to their situation. Usually, these descriptions are
vague and not direct. Thus, it can seemingly apply to everyone to who it
is targeted.

Another reason why cold reading is also so effective in analyzing what
people believe is because of the confirmation biases that people hold
today. This simply means that people absolutely love to dwell on memories that reinforce their own positions or favor them. Thus, they push out
things that might not really work well for them.

So when discussing with someone, you can pick up on these biases.
They usually lean towards these views by discussing things that might
not be clear but affirming it as being just that. These things or beliefs are
considered to be untouchable to these participants.

When mentalists detect these signals or beliefs, they will be able to
quickly understand several things about a person in a flash.

## Sub-Conscious Cold Reading Is the End Goal

When you start out trying to cold-read people, you are always going
to be conscious. If you aren't as observant, then you are going to miss

what you are looking for. However, once you have practiced well enough, you are going to notice something happening.

You are going to be able to read people without even trying. While this can sound exciting, it can also lead to several problems. The most obvious one is that it might make you less observant. If you are also trying to help someone understand themselves better, you might be assuming more based on what you think rather than the information your mind and observation have gathered.

The first step to getting there is to consider the various cold reading techniques. These techniques will help you establish a solid foundation for learning so much more.

## Different Techniques Used In Cold Reading

So here are some of the most trusted techniques in cold reading.

### 1. The Ruse of the Rainbow

Yes, get used to the weird names of the techniques because a few more will be revealed. The first technique is the rainbow ruse also called the ruse of the rainbow.

What this technique does is to state an obvious personality trait from someone and then narrow it down in the opposite direction. With this technique, the mentalist can open up a great range of potential traits and then narrow it down to what they actually mean.

While this will obviously be a trick, it will look pretty real to the participant. The truth is that every person has experienced both spectrums of emotions or personality traits. The mentalist will simply explore this to his or her advantage.

Here's a statement that illustrates this technique.

*"You look really gloomy right now and it seems you brood a lot. However, I know for a fact that there was a time when you were happy".*

When using the rainbow ruse, one of the best things to do is to mix things up. Using the same personality traits over and over again makes you look stale.

So, learn about many qualities and their opposite. Then, use them according to the particular situation you are dealing with.

It will work like a charm!

## 2. The Forer Effect

As previously mentioned, the Barnum effect or Forer effect plays a vital role in how cold reading goes. It appears regularly throughout this book too. It is definitely something that you should probably learn as early as possible. What the Forer effect does is that the mentalist says things to provoke a response from the participant. For example, a mentalist could say something that might allow the participant to follow patterns or connections with their lives.

When this happens, their eyes light up and they will probably be willing to fill in the gaps. The mentalist achieves this through the use of Barnum's statements. These statements as earlier mentioned seem to refer to just the participant. So, the participant is pretty shocked that the mentalist knows them that well.

In reality, the statement applies to so many people. It is not relative to just that participant. However, by doing so, mentalists make participants much more receptive. They also make them more readable.

The Barnum statement also allows them to fact-check many of their assumptions about the person. Once this happens, everything becomes so much clearer.

Here are some statements that a mentalist might say.

*"Your mom died from chest problems, didn't she?"*

Now, chest problems are really broad. This could be anything. However, at that moment, the participant is only so eager to affirm that thought and provide more information about the issues surrounding it.

By giving that general statement, the mentalist can confirm this knowledge, learn the real cause of death and even lead more. If you are a really good mentalist, this could be the start of an entirely new discovery.

### 3. The Art of Shotgunning

This is the most popular technique in cold reading. It might also be the first one you actually master. Just like a gun being fired at night towards a blurry target, the mentalist shoots a lot of information at a crowd of people.

When they do this, they then look for body language gestures, and actions. You will learn most of the body language gestures in the coming chapters.

Upon observing the reactions of the crowd, the mentalist then narrows his information according to a positive or negative reaction. The information that is provided can be anything. It can be positive, negative, rude, or even provocative.

To pull off this technique perfectly, you will need to learn everything you can about body languages and personality traits. Fortunately for us, this book has everything you need to know.

Here's an example of a statement that can be made when shotgunning.

*"I sense you loved someone in the past. You wish it worked out but it never stood a chance".*

Just imagine saying this in a room filled with at least 10 people. It's definitely going to resonate with almost half of the room. Once the mentalist sees this, he can then narrow down this broad information into something way more specific.

*"I sense you are dealing with a difficult situation right now".*

Once again, this is a very broad statement. Most people in life are always carrying one burden at a given time. When a mentalist tells this to a group of people, he will look out for signals such as interest, surprise, or a surge of hope. Any of these signals through human gestures will ensure that they can narrow it down even more. At the end of the day, the participants will feel like the mentalist has seen the depth of their soul.

## 4. Hot Reading and Other Techniques

You probably already wondered if hot reading exists. If you did, yes it does exist and it is quite the opposite of cold reading.

When it comes to hot reading, the mentalist already has a good idea of the knowledge on display and is simply trying to find out more.

The difference between cold and hot reading is that while cold reading depends solely on the responses of the participant to understand the situation, hot reading doesn't. Instead, it is already aware of the entire situation.

Thus, cold reading is much harder to execute than hot reading.

Another technique that can be used by mentalists is warm reading. This is right in the middle of cold and hot reading. The main difference here is that warm reading uses Barnum's statements to make a difference.

So, the art of warm reading is basically a combination of some of both the techniques listed here. It can be quite difficult to pull off at first. However, with some practice and consistency, you should be able to handle it with no problems.

## Tips on Perfecting Your Cold Reading Skills

Finally, we are going to look at some of the best tips you can follow to perfect your cold reading skills.

## 1. Start Small

It never hurts to start small. You are probably going to hear this a lot throughout this book. That's because it is the truth. Learn to start small and slowly grow.

Learning the techniques will take a while and that's okay. The bottom line is that you are slowly going to see the benefits of starting small. All you need is a dose of patience. Here is another thing that will definitely count.

## 2. Practice and More Practice

This will really depend on how far you can go and how fast you can get there. Truly, the more you practice, the better you are going to get at a particular technique.

So, just dedicate a specific time to practice. You can even get your close friends to practice with you. The thing about cold reading is that you can do it without the other party even knowing. However, don't make them feel weird, that just sucks!

## 3. Improve Your Observation Skills

If there is one skill you need to get the hang of this part of mentalism, it's observation. You have to be really observant. Most people find it really hard to hide how they feel especially when you take them by surprise. Use this to your advantage.

However, some people with certain personality traits are experts at making this happen. You will need your observation skills to detect even the smallest gestures they make and what they might mean.

With enough practice, it should be easy as pie!

# Conclusion

The art of cold reading is fundamental to mentalism. It is really the first step towards getting comfortable in this career. If you can get this part sorted out, you probably will be alright. However, you will need to learn about human behaviors and their gestures to pull them off.

# Chapter Four - Understanding Human Body Language

————

If there was anything we could think of that was older than language, what would that be? You could think of so many things. However, I'll give you one. Human body language. This allows humans to express themselves without even saying a word. This is often called non-verbal communication.

In the world of mentalism, the need to observe your participant closely is so important. That is the only way you can make valid assumptions and know their secret desires and motivations. In some cases, your participant might not be willing to tell you certain things about themselves. Humans tend to hide things really well when they are determined.

In such a situation, your best bet at uncovering the matter will be by understanding the body language of the person. That is easier said than done. There is so much to learn about human body languages and what they can mean.

This chapter will focus on the various body languages and what they can mean. By analyzing what they could mean, you allow yourself to learn a lot about human gestures and emotions. We will also look at how these gestures and emotions can influence their decisions in profound ways.

This chapter promises to have everything and more. You just have to stick around.

# The Power of Body Language

So, let's start from the top. Why do we think that body language has so much power? Let's see if we can break it down to make it easier to understand.

## 1. Body Language Holds Hidden Messages

If you were on a bus and an elderly person smiled at you, you subconsciously get a message or signal. That person is nice and cheerful. If someone is shaking or fidgeting, it's clear that the person is sad.

Those are very obvious body language. However, this is what it proves. It proves that you can read a message completely by just watching body language. It also shows that you can give a perfect response to the body language that you have witnessed. All you need is to be more observant.

## 2. It Breaks The First Barrier

Body language can be a really great way to break the barrier. This usually happens when two people meet each other for the first time. It is usually what people call a good first impression.

Have you ever just met someone and thought to yourself how unfriendly and unapproachable they are? Most times, the person in question never even spoke to you! Here's why you probably felt that way. Body languages. Perhaps you met the person and the person didn't bother to smile. Or maybe they smiled but their handshake was just a tad bit longer than usual.

Those are body language and can really set the tone for future impressions.

## 3. It Gives Away Bonds And Ties

Imagine meeting someone you know at a party or an event. Your body language is definitely going to give it away. If you are on pretty bad terms with the person, you might become cold and simply ignore the person. Others might tend to give the person a lot of space and avoid areas where the person can be found.

The bottom line is that body language can immediately tell you if people have certain ties and bonds with each other. They tell you just what you should know and quickly.

As a mentalist, this is crucial to learn your trade. You have to know when people are close to each other. This might help you read their intentions and motivations.

### 4. It Promotes Your Ability To Cold Read

As a mentalist, cold reading is one of the most important things you will learn. Cold reading is made easier by learning about body languages. As earlier stated, body language will ensure that you know who to narrow down your message to and the signals that they are emanating.

So, if you want to get really good at cold reading and pretty fast, then understanding body language is really not an option here.

## How Reliable Are Body Languages?

Now that we have made it absolutely clear that we must learn so much more about body languages, there are other matters we also have to discuss. One of them is definitely the reliability of the body language itself.

So how reliable is the human body language? To help understand just how much we can trust body languages, let's consider some of the most important things you should know about body languages.

### 1. The Face Can Be Deceiving

Most people who start out to learn about mentalism often make the mistake of looking at the participant's face. Most times, the face can be really deceiving.

Just think about it. Every day, people have to deal with so much stress and issues. Most times, these issues are with other humans. People have learned to mask their true feelings. Thus, they can keep their face neutral and a hidden mask when they want.

So, when you are trying to cold read or simply understand someone, never start with the face. Look for other signs. Trust me, there are so many others you can consider.

While this is true, the face is also a good giveaway. Sometimes, the shock or the surprise an action may bring will be too much for the participant. So, keep alert for any changes you might find.

## 2. Body Language Is Only About Signals And Intent

Here's another thing you have to understand about body language. It focuses mostly on intent and signals. There is nothing more to it. You cannot read the specific thoughts that people are having. You can only get a good estimate.

For example, when a person is attracted to someone else, their body language might give it away. However, you cannot really understand what that person's thoughts are. You can only understand the directions of the person's emotions.

Good mentalists learn to use this to narrow down messages and signals. The key is to use this emotional intent to fully understand what the person is thinking. In most cases, the person finally expresses those specific thoughts to you.

However, you will need to play your cards right to get to that level.

For the exact complexities of the art of reading body languages, there are so much more loopholes to exploit. Similar to the earlier stated example on how relatively easy it is for people to pick up signals of attraction, there is an even easier set of tells.

Because one of the most common or vital instincts is defensiveness, we will be focusing on that particular trait. We will pay a sufficient amount of information on how to unlock its secrets. How to tell if it's a defensive person could be complicated. Although, there are ways to tell who is defensive.

Engaging in a conversation with someone who sits with crossed legs or arms is the easiest tell of a defensive person.

But looking out for crossed legs or crossed arms is not all that is required to identify a defensive person. As a matter of fact, many are those who retain their defensive intents even though their legs or arms are "uncrossed". So, is there any hope in identifying their defensiveness? Well, it all comes down to the experience of the person involved.

There is no "one template fits all" approach. Those who are not used to hiding their feelings, tend to defend themselves by avoiding all others. What does this mean? They tend to avoid eye contact. While one might think that this is too basic, the elementary things are needed once in a while. It is among this type of defensive person that we find those who avoid by shifting their attention to other things.

The arms or legs crossing sends a relatively distinct message. That the person has everything under control and that not much explanation is needed when they are involved. It also means that you limit the amount of communication you are willing to give in that instant.

When interpreted, the few above paragraphs could be of importance in understanding defensive leaders. To fully appreciate the thoughtfulness and delicacy put into the creation, you have to open up one's mind to be freer. When one is more trusting, it is easier for such a person to figure out who not to trust. They can draw up a lot of comparisons and hence, make better decisions.

But as for the exact question bothering on the reliability of the human body language, there is a definite answer which will no doubt satisfy all parties involved. Human body language reading is a very much trustworthy aspect of communication. This is, however, restricted to those who know what to look out for.

The practicality of actually understanding the art of reading gestures and body language is generally quite versed. There are a lot of situations in which one eventually turns in their favor and entirely controls once they can get a read on the inner state of their audience.

So, from the work place to even personal homes and spaces, knowing the art of interacting with others can only ever bring benefits.

## Human Gestures and Mentalism

Gestures made by a person could be said to be one of the most reliable sources of body language "give away". This is because human gestures are unique to each and every one of us. So, while paying a sufficient amount of information, it is possible to catch slip-ups or hints people drop subconsciously.

Using gesture by itself is a science that has been studied by many over time. As a matter of fact, the parts of the human brain responsible for using and processing gestures have been identified. It is believed that numerous regions of the brain play a role here. Two of the more prominent ones include the 'Broca' and the 'Wernicke' region.

## History of Human Gestures

Interestingly, the use of gestures is believed to have evolved with the species. Scientists believe that using gestures among Homo sapiens evolved from an earlier form of communication (the gestural theory). This earlier system was similar to the current use of gestures. But at the time, using gestures was the major part of the communication system. Nowadays, gestures just sort of add color to speech. Identifying what figurative color has been added is the aim of numerous mentalist studies.

Typical examples of gestures include:

- Interlocking the fingers
- Small facial expressions (e.g., scrunching eyebrows in disapproval)
- Openly showing the palm of the hand to express unguardedness
- Nodding slightly by way of greeting
- Shrugging the shoulders in disinterest

- Making unconscious hand signs
- Tapping the fingers (either against other body parts or on objects)

The human gestures here are not the same thing as sign languages. Gestures are simply unconscious or at times conscious movements made to further reinforce or buttress certain parts of speeches.

If you want to know more about gestures, you should read chapter 8 of this book. It contains every single gesture you can think of and how a mentalist can twist it to their advantage.

## Applications of Human Gestures

These gestures on their own might be somewhat weird. However, once inserted into a speech, they make absolute sense.

For instance, imagine a man seemingly gesturing in the air using his hand. He does this with a frown on his face. If one sees a man doing this repeatedly, it would be a normal reaction to question the sanity of such a person. But imagine that same man giving a relatively passionate speech on the implications of say, global warming on our immediate environment. Then imagine that same man making the same gestures made earlier.

It is next to impossible that the man's sanity would be called to question any longer. Why is that? Because we finally understand what led to his gestures. While gestures might not always be that easy to understand or straightforward, we still need to look out for them. At this point, let us engage our imaginary capacities once more.

While A is giving a narrative or a speech, B, who was giving his undivided attention by leaning forward and remaining still, suddenly changes his posture. B initially relaxes into his seat. But this is not entirely bad because he might just feel like relaxing. But then, B rhythmically but slowly and quietly drops his fingers repeatedly on the table. This changes the message entirely.

The gesture of "drumming" his fingers on the table could be interpreted as a loss of interest. Assuming it is in a situation where the opinion of B matters to A, then it would be best to quickly summarize. Alternatively, A could bring out a trump card or essential information capable of totally recapturing every lost iota of attention by B.

This is just one very simple instance of understanding gestures. Not all gestures are so easy to pick up or understand. Hence the need to pay attention to one's audience will never be done away with. But at the same time, there are simple gestures that are just gestures. An example is a gesture made by our imaginary global warming speaker in the illustration earlier.

His gestures have no hidden meaning. He is simply pointing in the air. So there is a major need for discernment in understanding human gestures. One should be able to recognize when there is a hidden emotion in play. As well as when there is none. After all, some people just love to talk using hand gestures, nothing more.

Generally, it is easy to identify or figure out the emotion behind certain human gestures. The difficult part lies in actually identifying which gesture has a hidden meaning and which one does not. This means that to understand a gesture, one has to first understand to a certain extent the person using the gesture.

At this point, we could rightly conclude that there are personalized as well generalized gestures. For personalized gestures, one would need to be well acquainted with another person to get a full grasp of the person's tells. This is the basis upon which the slightest movement of the eyes could make two people burst into laughter. This often happens between best friends.

But this is not an exclusive principle. Being highly observant of those around could help a person get decently acquainted with others quickly. But other than this, one could also get acquainted with generalized tells. These could vary based on location or they could remain the same as everywhere else.

Regardless of the particular circumstance, it would be more than beneficial to pay attention to human gestures. This is particularly beneficial for those who are regularly in contact with others. From HR (human resources) staff to those from educational or medical sectors, no one is particularly exempted.

## Human Emotions and Mentalism

Human emotions are the most unique aspects of humans. Some believe that emotions are all a person is. A human being is made up of and driven by dozens or even hundreds of complex emotions and feelings. These feelings could at times be overwhelming but they are an essential part of our lives as humans. The most powerful types or forms of inter-person relationships seem to be those built on emotional grounds.

This is just one aspect of human lives that shows the importance of human emotions. It seems that most, if not all decisions we make are based on emotions. Even for those who claim to make unbiased decisions, there is almost definitely a hint of involvement of emotions.

The most central emotions in humans are love and hate or like and dislike. All other emotions seem to be derivatives of these two. Those emotions similar to hate could manifest themselves as things or elements that we are uncomfortable with. Emotions in this category could range from disgust to fear or terror.

As for the derivatives of love we have so many of them. Happiness or contentment, empathy, sympathy are just a few examples. All these emotions play a large role in our lives as humans and in the decisions we make. Their effect could be conscious or unconscious, large or small.

## Universal Emotions

All these emotions appear on different scales in various individuals. This is what makes us all unique as humans. These emotions, when recognized and carefully handled, make it easier to relate with people. But is it truly possible to be able to get acquainted with all manifestations of emotions in everyone? The answer is no!

This is where the issue of universal emotions comes in. The fact that these emotions are referred to as universal does not mean that they are the most important or vital ones in our lives. However, it means that a lot of people spend their time wearing one of these emotions.

As humans, we can be described as being genetically wired to show our emotions. After all, if that wasn't the case why would our faces have no less than 43 different muscles? But that is not the most awesome aspect. In reality, we can make as many as 10 000 different expressions. Want to know something even more awesome?

These expressions that our faces can display were not taught. Supposedly they trace back to our primitive or primordial roots. Which makes perfect sense! After all, who taught anyone how to express fear? And how come even newborns express fear or dread in the same way an adult would, with a shudder and in extreme cases a scream or cry?

Regardless of the variations that might have naturally occurred to make each individual's expressions somewhat unique, some emotions are common. These universal emotions transcend race, time, and personal beliefs. They are said to be seven in number. They are:

## 1. Fear

We will be starting with fear because it seems to be the most universal and unchanging emotion among humans everywhere. It starts with a shiver through the bones, with hair standing straight and pupils dilated. These are the basic signs and tells of a scared and or petrified person. Fear as a human emotion could be said to be the most primitive one. Identifying the look or expression of fear should be a relatively easy task.

This is because, at one point or another, everyone on the planet must have related to the emotion of fear. Hence it should not be difficult to identify its signs in others we run into in our day-to-day lives.

The expression of fear contains all that we need in that situation. This is because fear is never alone. Humans have the fight or flight reflex. This means that while scared it is almost impossible not to be tense. We are tense because the body prepares us to either fight or run.

## 2. Anger

The feeling of almost figuratively blowing up. The intake of oxygen seems to exponentially multiply as one prepares to lash out. Anger is expressed in a simple way, similar to fear. Once a person is successful in analyzing someone else, understanding when the said "someone" is angry is not rocket science.

There are a few tells such as the typical tightening of fists or the obvious raising of the voice. Dealing with others also requires that a person knows how to navigate other people's anger. We should be able to notice early signs and take appropriate steps to avoid or manage said anger.

## 3. Contempt

This emotion is one that no one would want to be directed at them. Put simply, it is the emotion emitted when one looks down on someone else. The person holds no regard for the other one. In a way, the expression of contempt has been said to be a hybrid borne out of the mixture of anger and distrust.

That smug look that everyone hates is the most vivid expression of contempt. However, in its most hidden expression, it could be seen as a slight upward curve from the side of the lip.

## 4. Surprise

Here, the most obvious expression of this emotion is a dilation of pupils as well as a slight opening of the mouth, usually left hanging. It is one of the briefest expressions, but its effects could be relatively long-lasting. A good surprise makes one happy whenever the thought comes up. An unpleasant surprise leaves a bitter aftertaste whenever it is remembered.

## 5. Disgust

This is evidently manifested by a world-renowned wrinkling or scrunching of the nose. Interestingly, there is scientific backing for that expression. As we squint our eyes, it prevents unknown particles from entering. And the scrunching of the nose minimizes the entry of unpleasant odor. It is an extreme dislike.

## 6. Sadness

This particular expression seems to have its aura. Once one sees a sad person, it is almost impossible not to know or notice. The emotion of sadness is almost contagious.

## 7. Happiness

The emotion of happiness rests on the opposite end of the scale from sadness. When one is genuinely happy, they carry a smile that makes everyone else want to smile. As long as a person does not have a personal issue with a smiling person, there is a high possibility that the smile could transfer.

## Understanding Human Motivations

Human emotions and gestures are probably some of the most exciting things to look forward to. However, there is one other category that we would like to mention. That is human decision-making.

Now, I know what you are thinking. You are probably wondering how this even relates to mentalism and understanding what people secretly desire. If this is you, then you are probably looking at things from the wrong angle.

Human decisions are often made based on two broad reasons. One of them is cold hard logic while the other is emotions. Sometimes, these decisions are a mixture of both. Other times, it might be as a result of various circumstances.

For example, everyone you meet has an underlying desire or motivation that drives them to succeed. This can be behind the decisions that they make and when they make them.

We will now seek to understand how people behave when they make decisions made on these factors. We shall do this by first understanding the various motivations and how to show them.

## How to pick up on the motivations of other people

So, here are some of the best motivators of people.

### 1. The Need for Power

This is by far one of the greatest motivations. The need for power did not start now. For years, people started wars based on the need to expand their power. Civilizations have fallen because several important people have fought viciously for power.

Just think of Alexander the Great and his army chiefs who divided up his land after his death. The best way to spot someone who wants power and loves power is in their speech. These people are the ones that do not want to be controlled by others.

So, most decisions they make are going to be heavily influenced by this trait. Understanding this will allow you to deal with them better.

### 2. Competition

While we all have a bit of competition in us, some people are really competitive. They simply want to be the best in what they do. So, having someone else challenging them might be a great motivator.

However, a competitive spirit when taken to the extreme can also be the catalyst for serious issues. For example, people who are competitive to an extreme can be violent and commit certain crimes.

Often, displaying a competitive spirit could be due to the fact that they attach their self-worth to such being ahead of everyone else.

Note that competitiveness in this sense is completely different from self-improvement. The difference is in the motivations once again.

Someone interested in self-improvement might be ahead of others. However, their motivation is about improving themselves and not being ahead of others.

## 3. Building a Legacy

For others, the idea of being forgotten after they have died might be very taunting. So, they do all they can to build up a legacy that will last for years after their passing.

This determination will influence the decisions they make and their attitudes towards several concepts and beliefs. For these ones, nothing will make them happier than to have a legacy built in their name.

## 4. Independence

Some people are motivated by the lure of independence. They want to experience true freedom. This might play a big part in their decision-making process.

This type of people will see traditional concepts as less appealing. They will want to work flexible hours as well as do things their own way.

As a mentalist, you can easily spot someone craving independence by looking at the history of their decisions.

Combine this with some Barnum or shotgunning methods and you should have all the answers you want.

## 5. Making an Impact

Another core motivation will be to make an impact. This can be done through the workplace, a relationship, or in the world in general.

Regardless of the type of impact they make, people will only feel satisfied once they achieved this.

This type of person might make huge sacrifices to meet their goals and quests.

There are so many other things that can serve as motivators to people. From career progression to money, the list is endless.

It's your job as a mentalist to figure out what motivates people. There are good reasons why you should do this too.

## Importance Of Knowing People's Motivation As A Mentalist

### 1. It Makes The Job Easier

To know what people secretly want or desire, you have to know some information about them. This helps make cold reading a lot faster.

Knowing what motivates people is one of the fastest ways to pinpoint their desires. You should know that they will vary depending on the various circumstances of the situation.

However, as a mentalist, you will definitely want to be armed with such information early on.

### 2. It Allows You To Read Their Body Languages Properly

Throughout this chapter, we have talked at length about human emotions and how it affects their gestures. If there is something that can make you even better at reading such body language, then it's knowing people's motivators.

Gestures that signal defensiveness or being uncomfortable will be far easier to spot when you know their motivations.

### 3. It Allows You To Build Bonds And Connections With Your Participants

If you are going to be a mentalist, you will need to put your participants at ease. In some situations, this can be easy to do. Sometimes, they won't even know. However, in other situations, people might try to mask their emotions and keep a low profile.

Building the right connections might be easier once you know what motivates people. Chances are that the person is also very passionate about those things.

So, if you can drive the conversation from the angle of their motivations, chances are that you are going to see significant progress and fast.

### 4. Motivations Define People's Lives

Here's another good reason why you should take people's motivations seriously. It can define their entire life. The truth is that everything we do in life is for a purpose or is motivated by something else. These motivations are all part of a bigger lifelong motivation.

So, our whole life is being pushed in a certain direction. For example, a person who is motivated by the need to be comfortable financially will likely aim for financial independence, by just defining people's motivations, we will be able to know exactly what they want in life. That may help you understand them better.

## So how can you read people's minds effectively?

Well, the entire purpose of this book to use mentalism is to know what people secretly want or desires. So how can you make this happen efficiently?

### Don't Panic

It can be a rollercoaster when you first try out these new skills. However, the key here is not to panic. There are so many things you still have to learn. So, if your best efforts don't seem to be working well, just know that it's a matter of time. While it's perfectly normal for you to feel disappointed, never give up. If you have reached this chapter, you have already come too far along to quit.

## Practice Understanding human behaviors

The key to being a great mentalist is knowing what each human gesture or action means. That can only be possible if you practice. So, make out time to consciously look out for these skills. The good thing about mentalism is that you do not need to be restrained in a room to learn.

You can learn so much by just interacting with others in your everyday life. You will be able to spot all the gestures and actions we have identified and understand their meaning.

So, never switch off when you are with others!

## Know it takes time

Yes, I'm pretty sure you have heard this before. However, I am going to say it again. It takes time to actually understand humans and their body language. They are very complex and one body language can mean several things.

So, understand that it can take time before you become an expert in this category. I'd recommend that you slowly work your way up. Start from the easier gestures and actions. Things will get easier from then on.

## Stay Committed

Finally, stay committed to your end goal. The goal here is to be a great mentalist with an exceptional understanding of how people function. You want to understand their secret desires. So, stay committed to that work.

You'll definitely get there!

## Conclusion

So there we are! Now, we know people's body language and the signals they might be giving off. Next, we shall consider how you can read the intentions of people. Knowing the intentions of individuals will only make your readings more accurate as a mentalist.

# Chapter Five - The Art of Reading People's Intentions

———

The human mind is a complex web. Despite being invisible, it has a strong influence on a person's personality. Just as our faces are different so are our minds as well. People's minds work differently. Your ability to read a person's mind effectively and successfully will enhance the quality of your relationship.

When you understand how a person's mind works, you will know how to deal with them. It will determine if a new relationship will continue or suffer an early death. Your ability to read people's minds will help you ascertain if a person is genuine or not.

When you understand how a person interacts with the world, you won't get offended by something they do. Learning to effectively read a person's mind will aid communication and comprehension. It will also help to reduce the rate of strife and quarrel in a relationship. The ability to read people's minds is an important skill that should be mastered by all.

Most importantly, knowing people's minds and their intentions will make you a good mentalist. That, to us is really the most important thing.

In this chapter, we'll explore the different ways a person's personality can be determined within seconds of interacting with them.

# How to Detect a Liar within Seconds of Interaction

It is a universal truth that no one enjoys being lied to. Even when the reason for the lie is to shield them from harm's way, most people will rather deal with the truth than cope with the lies. Often, the first sign that someone is lying to you is the inconsistency in their story. It can be hard for them to keep up with their lies.

However, some people have trained themselves so well in the art of lying that it becomes difficult to detect when they are actually lying to you or telling the truth. Since these liars have honed their craft in lying, why shouldn't you hone your craft in detecting them within seconds of interaction?

As unpleasant as lying might be, the majority of us have lied at one point or another. Even you have lied before. Maybe you lied this morning. A lie must not be so serious to qualify as a lie. Telling your friend or neighbor that their outfit is nice even when you do not agree, is a lie! The truth has been altered, a person has been deceived.

No matter how hard we try, people will always tell lies. Some of these lies will go undetected or only get noticed when it is too late. However, if you know how to read the signs of a liar, you won't always fall for their traps. All liars attempt to conceal the truth using certain patterns, but the mind never forgets and that's our secret to uncovering the truth.

The beautiful thing about the human mind is that it can never be lied to. It always knows the truth and never forgets, no matter how hard you try to do so. For a liar to sustain their lies to the point where you fall for their lies, they need to train their mind to obey and follow a certain pattern. It is these various patterns that we'll be exploring in this chapter.

As a mentalist, your duty will always be to spot patterns between people's utterances. Knowing these patterns will allow you to spot when they are telling a lie. Here are some ways to easily spot a liar.

## 1. Start With the Right Questions

The first step to finding out if a person is a lying or not is to make them comfortable around you. Asking simple and nonthreatening questions reduces their tension and allows them to lower their guard around you. Since they won't willingly give up the truth, you'll have to trick their mind to get the cat out of the bag.

Ask those questions you know will provide truthful responses, questions within their safe zone. You can ask questions about the weather, their health, or any other innocent question that won't put them on the edge. The aim of asking these questions is to observe their language when they're comfortable and telling the truth.

You should listen to the tone of their voice, how they gesticulate, their facial expressions, and general body movements. This will give you a picture of their composure when they're telling the truth and allow you to juxtapose it with any change you observe in the course of your interaction with them.

## 2. Explore the Forbidden Zone

The forbidden zone is that part of a liar's life they do not wish to bring to the limelight. Simply because a person lies doesn't mean they want to always alter the truth. They'll rather prepare their lie in case of any emergency. As oxymoronic as this might sound, liars, do not wish to have to tell a lie to anyone but end up lying as a means to an end.

Now that you've lowered their guard and you've earned a shred of their trust, it's time to explore the forbidden zone. At this point, you will still be asking simple questions, but questions you suspect will elicit a lie.

When a person is asked a question that will require them to conceal the truth, they use the initial microseconds to put up their defense. These microseconds serve as your window of opportunity to ascertain whether or not a person is a liar.

Because you started your interactions with them on an innocent footing, they didn't prepare their mind for when you'll explore the forbidden zone. Now they're struggling with interacting with you and keeping up with their lies. This discomfort causes an alteration in their general body language, voice tone, facial expressions, and gesticulations.

The difference between a skilled liar and an everyday liar is the amount of time they spend putting up their defense. No matter how skillful a liar is, when caught off balance they'll always be surprised. When exploring the forbidden zone, make sure you don't ask direct questions or questions that will scare them away.

Once you're done with your questioning, compare the reactions you got from asking innocent questions with the ones you got from exploring their forbidden zone. They can tell the story a million times but because their mind knows the truth, they can't emphasize their point. If you are observant enough, a lot of lies won't go undetected by you.

Liars tend to know what to say to cover up their tracks but they fail to fully master the emotional expressions that can go with their lies. Because the story they're telling is an alteration of the truth, they fail to emphasize what they're saying.

## The Unspoken Words of a Handshake

Handshaking is a practice as old as time. There are records of ancient artworks that show people shaking hands. Handshakes are a friendly way of greeting people and assuring them that you come in peace. It bridges the gap of the language barrier, the gap of racism and sexism, and any other social division that exists in the world. Handshakes silently say, "I accept you" or "I welcome you".

Some sports such as football and boxing require the competitors to shake hands before and after a game. This shows proper sportsmanship and an indication that the competing parties promise to remain civil throughout the game. Handshakes are a sign of trust.

Asides from sports, handshakes are being used in the corporate world to start and end a meeting; they are also used when deals are being closed. They are used in politics after an election result is announced.

Handshakes are also employed in our everyday life; we use handshakes to greet both acquaintances and friends. We shake those we accept.

People often use your handshake style to form their initial opinion of you. Even though handshakes are generally believed to be a sign of peace and an establishment of a cordial relationship, is that always the case?

What exactly does a person's handshake say about their personality?

A handshake goes beyond holding hands and acting nice. If you are observant, you can tell a thing or two about the personality of the person who you are shaking the hand. You can tell if they are confident, scared, agitated, intimidated, threatened, calm, or disrespectful. Handshakes may not have mouths but they sure do have voices and never hesitate to communicate with the palm of the other person.

To understand the personality of the person you are greeting with a handshake, you must learn to observe and read simple bodies. Here are some handshaking styles and what they say about a person.

- **The Double Hand Shaker**

These people shake you with both hands. Often they give a half-bow whilst shaking one of your hands with both of theirs. This is a sign of respect to you. It shows that they consider you their superior and accept your dominance.

It is also a mark of humility from a superior authority. This means that even if they are superior to you, they respect you and acknowledge the fact that you also have something to offer. Irrespective of how little your contribution might be, they'll welcome it. These types of individuals consider who their shaking hands with to be equal, regardless of their age, gender, or social status.

This handshake can also serve as a defense mechanism. The person who is shaking you does not trust you and is attempting to incapacitate you by putting their second hand over your hand.

You can understand the nature of their personality from the environmental setting. The double-handed shake will mean different things

63

depending on the setting. This handshake is a sign that a person is confident in their ability, so they don't need to prove any point to you.

- **The Superior Hand Shaker**

These people ensure that when they shake your hand, their hands are over yours. This set of people believe that they are superior to you and they want you to also know this. Their grasp may be strong and their shake aggressive. This is a sign of power. Their shake silently says "I'm in-charge and you should know this". This type of handshake attempts to establish the boundaries of the relationship.

Most times, these types of people are either bullies or insecure fellows who attempt to hide their insecurity by being aggressive towards others. They may be condescending. They believe that dominance must be shown through force or action. This handshake points towards a person being arrogant.

- **The Shy or Submissive Hand Shaker**

These people are naturally shy or easily intimidated. Their hands are usually under yours and their grasp is weak and their shake quickly or fast. This type of handshake silently says "you are the boss and I know that". They tend to say little or nothing and avoid eye contact.

These types of people are easy to control or intimidate because they have naturally conceded to the fact that you are superior to them. So they won't put up a fight when you attempt to establish dominance. Often, these people are just scared of you and find it hard to conceal their fear. Your presence sends chills down their spine.

- **The Casual Shaker**

This set of people don't attach much importance to shaking hands or don't care about your perception of them. They do not hold your hands fully and often give a casual handshake. This kind of handshake is neither disrespectful nor reverential. It is more of an "I-recognize-your-presence" kind of shake and is mostly reserved for our peers.

A person's handshake can only give you an idea of who they might be, but that doesn't mean that's how they are. Maybe you met them on one of their bad days or good days. In essence, never judge a person's character solely based on the nature of their handshake. There is more to a person than their handshake.

## How the Legs Reveal the Secret of the Mind

The legs reveal so much information about the mind of a person. However, legs are often overlooked in the study of body language. We don't fully appreciate the message the legs of a person attempts to pass. The problem is that we've restricted the function of the legs to just locomotion.

The movements of the legs provide information on a person's state of mind and true intention faster than any other part of the body. This is why it can be used in the study of deception and lies.

A person's legs can reveal anger, pain, sadness, depression, excitement, misery, anxiety, fear, nervousness, intimidation, authority, confidence, tiredness, disappointment, comfort, discomfort, shame, pride, surprise, disgust, tension, urgency and so much more.

The legs immediately respond to any threat or excitement. The brain is in constant communication with the legs. It's the brain that perceives what is happening in the environment and alerts the legs of any need to run or stop.

If you're given a surprise birthday gift, chances are you'll start jumping and walking about the place. Imagine walking home alone from work in the evening and some creepy fellow is following you. You'll be scared and your pace will increase. If you can't control your fear you might end up breaking into a run.

### Why?

Your mind perceives danger and your legs simply comply with the wishes of your mind to leave that vicinity. This is why there is an adrenaline rush, to help you escape.

Another example of how the leg movements demonstrate our state of mind is when we are awaiting the announcement of a result. You so are

65

eager to find out what the outcome will be that you unconsciously begin to shake your legs. These leg movements demonstrate anxiety.

What about when you are very angry and you stamp your feet on the ground? Your stamping demonstrates your frustration. The feet and leg movements often express a person's current state of mind. It shares important pieces of information about a person and the nature of their personality.

If you are observant, you'll notice that there is a difference between the stride of an influential person and that of a pauper; the stride of an honest person and that of a bank robber escaping the crime scene.

The difference between the movements of the leg and other parts of the body like our face and hands is that the legs are honest and defiant. A lot of people have mastered the art of masking their true facial expression and their voice tone but the legs have proven tough to master. So you are utterly disgusted by a person's behavior but because you have to act nice, you wear a smile.

You are completely pissed about a situation but in the course of talking about your displeasure, you never once raised your voice. You wear a calm expression all through the course of an argument because showing your anger may be considered uncivil or disrespectful (if you're angry at an older person).

The legs don't care whose ox is gored, if they don't like a thing they express it. If they're happy about the outcome of a situation, they express it. If they're frustrated with a situation, they express it. Until you stop placing so much importance on the other body expressions, excluding the legs, you won't adequately understand a person's state of mind.

Even the feet and leg expression of a liar speaks. So when their face is pretending to be innocent, their legs are ratting them out to whoever cares to observe them. No matter how skilled a liar is, they initially lose control of their composure when they are on the verge of being caught.

Even though the legs pass some vital information about the true intentions of a person; it isn't the only factor that should be looked at. The point I'm trying to make is, the legs shouldn't be neglected in the study of body language. There's more to it than just walking somewhere.

## The Magic of a Smile

A smiling face is a friendly face. The more you smile, the more people tend to attract. You'll only ask a grumpy person for directions if you can't find a smiling person. A smile is a non-verbal way of saying "you are welcome", "you are free to feel comfortable around me", "I'm happy" or "life is good and I have no worries". A person who smiles a lot tends to have more friends than a grumpy person.

Smiling is associated with a lot of perks and people tend to treat you differently when you smile. In some cultures, smiling is a must when welcoming guests to your home or community. It shows that you accept these guests into your home and frowning is considered disrespectful. Socially, people are expected to smile because it is nice to smile. You are expected to smile for a photograph.

Smiling has become both a social and cultural norm, it is almost mandatory in some settings. Whether you're happy or not, provided you work at the customer service of any organization, you must always wear a smile.

In a bid to get accepted by society, people feign a smile all the time. It is as if the world says to you, «irrespective of what goes on in your life, you must smile! Else people won't come close to you. " It is imposed on you and if you dare to defy the laws of society, your consequence is loneliness.

People pretend to be happy when they're not. Pretend to want people around when they just want to be left alone. Smiling when you should be grieving over some misfortune that has befallen you is seen as a mark of strength. The fear of being perceived as weak forces people to smile.

So much negativity is associated with being a grumpy person. Grumpy people are often shunned or feared. People don't always know how to deal with an 'angry face'. People tend to negatively misjudge you when you frown.

Also, because smiling is generally believed to be the mark of a good person, a lot of predators smile. They wear a smile when they go hunting for their prey. They need their prey to believe that they are good people. When these people don't consider the predator a threat, they tend to lower their guard around them. Instead of fleeing, these preys go close because they trust that they won't be harmed.

Smiling can be a good thing but it can also be a danger zone. The mind doesn't naturally perceive a smiling face as a threat at first glance. A smile can give you an idea of the personality of the person you're dealing with. There are some signs you can look out for to ascertain if a person is wearing a genuine smile or is only covering up some top secret.

- **Smiling Excessively**

Now, it isn't bad to smile! Smiling is a human right. However, when a person smiles excessively, it is often because they're hiding something. When a person smiles at things they have no business smiling at, it only shows that they're hiding something.

They may or may not be hiding some heinous plan on how to destroy humanity. They may just be sad and are trying to pretend to be fine so that they don't burden you with their problems. A sad person smiles excessively because they believe that if they don't smile, you'll see through them. An evil person smiles excessively when their plan is going just as planned.

- **The Smirk or Half-Smile**

Naturally, people smile with every muscles in their face but a person smirks with only the lip muscle. A person might smirk because they're planning something evil or they aren't impressed by the joke. They could also wear a half-smile because they are expected to act nice but wish they can be mean.

A smirk can also serve as an indication of fatigue. They are genuinely fascinated by the joke or occurrence but are too tired to adequately express their fascination.

The truth is, you can't use just a smile to ascertain if a person is genuine or not. To fully understand the personality of who you are dealing with, you need to study them alongside their other body languages. Every aspect of their body language works hand-in-hand.

## Signals and Gestures That Signal Courtship

Once in a while, we're attracted to people and we wish for them to know that we are attracted to them. We make affectionate gestures towards them because we want them to notice us. Our attitude changes immediately once they're around the vicinity because we want to impress them. We want them to consider us sophisticated and worth their while.

This attraction exists across all species. Courtship encourages reproduction by initiating mating. The universe requires all biological species to reproduce for the sake of continuity. Most times courtship aims to establish a long-term relationship with the person you find attractive. Often it's the need for companionship that leads to this attraction.

The human courtship behaviors are different and more sophisticated than that of other species. If the aim of courtship is marriage, courtship signals are expected to be established and maintained.

When you're attempting to establish a courtship with an individual you are attracted to, you need to show them that you are interested in them. Males and females of every species display different traits that signal courtship. For the sake of the subject matter, we'll just stick to how we signal courtship.

- **The Male Courtship Gestures**

The human male attempts to display his quality when a female approaches. In his attempt to showcase his traits, he is expected to follow some socially accepted rules. For example, a man is not expected to grab a woman by her breast or buttocks on their first encounter. No matter how attractive that woman might find him, such actions will most likely turn her off.

The man is expected to exhibit superiority in certain aspects of his life. He is expected to demonstrate his superior qualities when he is around the person he wishes to attract. The traits that will get him noticed are determined by the person's preferences.

For example, a woman might want an intellectually sound man but not be bothered by his stature. Another woman might want a physically built man and will not mind if he isn't intellectually sound. Different strokes for different folks!

In most cultures, the man is expected to chase after the female. It is believed that the outcome of a courtship signal is determined by the female. If she doesn't find him attractive, she repels him until he stops coming after her or if she is impressed by his persistence.

Research has shown that it is culturally and socially expected that a man is direct about his attraction. He is to show this through verbal and non-verbal gestures. He can be aggressive about his intentions, but not in a way that is considered socially repulsive.

- **The Female Courtship Signals**

In some cases, the woman finds a particular person attractive. In this situation, she is expected to put out some signals to get the person's attention. Women are also expected to display their many quality features.

Some traditions and cultures frown upon women being direct about their attraction towards other people, particularly men. However, women are still expected to attract their partners. Some cultures and societies go as far as shunning the lady when she isn't able to attract a worthy suitor or partner. The woman then has to employ non-verbal and non-aggressive means to attract the partner she wants.

If you live in western countries, this is most likely not relatable.

Women are being direct about their intentions towards people they find attractive. They're employing verbal and non-verbal measures to attract the right partners.

No matter the gender, courtship signals have to deal with putting out signals that you're interested in a person. The person then decides whether or not to consider your offer of courtship. Sending out signals isn't bad and is socially acceptable. It only becomes a problem when the attracted party attempts to use force or emotional blackmail to get what they want.

## How to Use Non-Verbal Cues To Influence and Read People

Human communication goes beyond speech. A person can communicate their message through body language. For instance, if a person is horny and wishes to have sex with their partner, they don't always have to express their feelings with words. Body language and non-verbal cues can do the trick.

A person's voice tone, facial expression, actions, and body posture are strong tools of non-verbal communication. They can let people know what you can condone and what you can't tolerate. You can also use non-verbal means of communication to pass messages you do not wish to communicate verbally.

One of the primary keys to a successful relationship, be it intimate or cordial, is communication. It mustn't always be verbal. Provided a message has been passed by one part and understood by the other, communication has occurred. The body can help you build stronger and healthier relationships both professionally and personally.

Non-verbal cues and communications speak the loudest. Whether you're aware of it or not, each time you interact with a people, you give off and receive some wordless energy. These cues could attract them or chase them away. Understanding the cues you give off can help you influence people. You can easily influence people when you send out the right message.

Most times, these non-verbal cues are sent out based on impulse. Your body automatically sends out the message it believes needs to be sent out to keep you safe. So if a person terrifies you, your body language and non-verbal cues fear. If you're comfortable or not comfortable around a person, your non-verbal cues express this.

Consciously or not, we act upon the wordless signals we receive from people. So if you wish to establish a friendship with a person and your "hello" is met with a frown, you'll certainly stay away. Their action has shown you that they aren't interested in your friendship request. Interestingly, even when we speak our non-verbal cues send out more information.

Non-verbal cues are more honest than our words; they're the voice of the mind. They don't attempt to impress anyone and this is why they're so loud despite not having a voice of their own. Behavioral psychology studies non-verbal cues.

If you're observant, you'll notice that a person's non-verbal actions can inform you of their true intentions. How they stare at you; how their voice rises and falls; and the passion with which they speak of a subject, can all express what their truth is.

The importance of non-verbal cues cannot be overemphasized; here are some advantages of observing a person's non -verbal cue:

- They can be used to emphasize what is being said. The passion in a person's eyes and the authority with which they speak convey more information than what is being said.

- The body language can also contradict what is being said. For example, a neighbor seeks your opinion about their outfit, because you're trying to be nice you say it is fine. If you're lying and you think the outfit is terrible, your non-verbal cues will expose your lies. If you have poor control of your laughter or they just look ridiculous, you may start laughing. Also, the study of psychology has shown that if a person's mouth says "yes" but their head says "no" and vice versa, that person might be lying.

- Non-verbal communication can be used in situations where words can't adequately convey the message. For example, you admire a dress but can't find the words to use to describe how lovely it is, your non-verbal cues will send the message.

Non-verbal cue is simply the unanimous agreement of some critical body parts and physical gestures. These could include:

## Eye Contact

The eyes say a thousand things the mouth is too scared to say. A person's eyes can express admiration or disgust, whilst the mouth says another. Maintaining eye contact can also help sustain the flow of a conversation.

## Posture

A person's poise can express confidence or timidity. It can show how they feel at any given time. Your posture can also express fatigue, depression, anxiety, fear, disappointment etc.

## Touch

Touch can communicate affection. It can also be used to communicate sexual attraction and desire. Touch can also express perversion, it can give a person the idea that they are in harm's way or a person has malicious intentions.

## Space

A clingy person can be very creepy. Sometimes people need space, especially when they barely know you. Imagine a guy walking up to you at the ATM and standing near you. Your defense mechanism will be activated and your body will go into a 'fight-or-flight' mode.

## Intonation

The rise and fall of your voice if you are angry, happy, sad, and miserable or you just wish to be left alone. It can also tell if you're pleased or underwhelmed by a person's presence.

# Tips to follow when trying to read people

If there is one thing that all humans have in common, it is the need to build strong and healthy relationships. We can never truly know the intentions of people when we first meet them, but we can attempt to read them. Here are some tips to follow when trying to read people:

1. Listen to what they say and the jokes they make. If you're attentive enough, you'll get a mental picture of the kind of person they are and what believe they hold sacred. Just learn to listen more than you talk. Talk about things that concern the subject under discussion.

2. Pattern never lies, people do! Often, people attempt to impress us with their words and actions. They believe that by telling us what they think we want to hear, they can prove that they're good people. Their non-verbal actions will always rat them out, you just need to observe.

3. Never rush the process of friendship, let it unravel itself naturally.

4. Observe how people treat that the ones they cannot benefit anything from. This paints a picture of who they truly are and not who they say they are.

5. Listen to the nature of the words they use. Are they subtle with their choice of words or vulgar?

6. Is their story consistent or not?

7. How do they gesticulate when they're comfortable and how does their body respond to discomfort?

8. How do they walk? Do they walk with grace and style or are they timid?

9. What feeds their ego?

10. What discussions do they enjoy?

11. How do they deal with disappointment or disagreement?

12. Are they quick to anger, or does their voice go up when they aren't getting what they want?

## Conclusion

Understanding the intentions of people and what goes on their head is important to the mentalist journey.

At this point, we are almost done comparing and understanding how humans behave and what this could mean to a mentalist. We now want to look at yet another important area.

That area has to deal with personality differences and how it affects people's desires and intentions.

# Chapter 6 - How Personality
# Differences Affect Mentalism

————

Mentalism insists on the position that there is a mental phenomenon, in reality, such mental phenomena include thinking and feeling. Mentalism also stands in its position that it can not be reduced to just a psychological or physical phenomenon such as reductionism suggests.

The term mentalism is sometimes used in place of idealism, and even though some kinds of mentalism maintain the position that it can not be reduced to just physical entities, it is established in physical processes.

Referring to mentalism, the psychology of mentalism puts its focus on thought process and perception. Good examples of thought process and perception could include cognitive psychology such as mental imagery, consciousness, and cognition.

But you already know all that good stuff. Cognitive psychology eventually brought about the study of personality and other related areas.

In this chapter, we shall be looking at the meaning of personality traits, the various types of personalities and their differences.

## Origin and Understanding the Meaning of Personality

What is personality and where does it come from? Does it come naturally? Does it change as we grow or does it remain the same? Questions such as these have led to a lot of theories that grew with the help of psychology.

It is important to note that psychologists do not exactly agree on a particular definition of the term personality. However, it is described broadly as the characteristics structure of our thoughts, feelings, and behaviors that makes a person distinctive.

It is not surprising that researchers have been able to determine why we have the personality that we have. Researchers have also been able to determine why some things can influence our personality. Even though some aspects of our personality might change as we get older, in many cases, the main aspects of our personality tend to remain consistent throughout our life.

Sense of personality is such an important part of our life, an entire branch of psychology is devoted to studying the mind-blowing topic. The psychologist that study personality and personality traits do so with special interest in individuals. They also carry out studies on personality similarities among large or small groups.

## Can Personality Traits be influenced?

For us to fully understand mentalism and why people act the way they do, we would need to learn some key things in understanding how personality works. Here are some factors that might influence our personality traits:

### It Can Be Influenced By The Current Situation

Individuals may express some aspects of their personality in different situations. These responses are generally predictable.

### It Can Be Influenced By The Environment

Though stable, our personality can be influenced by the environment. A good example is when having a shy personality. Being in an emergency situation might push you to take up a more outspoken countenance and take charge.

Behaviors are a result of personalities. The way you react to people and objects around you is usually based on the type of personality you have. Your personality also affects your choices with regards to career or every other part of your life.

The term personality refers to a particular way of feeling, thinking or behaving. Personality might encompass our attitude, our moods, our opinions, and how they are expressed. The way we interact with people around us shows or reflects the type of personality we have.

Our behavioral traits are part of our personality. This includes behaviors we learned or those that we were born with. Those behaviors differentiate one person from another and can be noticed in how people relate socially and with their environment.

Personality has been defined in many ways, but in psychology, there have been two main explanations for personality:

1.  It refers to the regular differences that stand between people. So this particular study of personality is focused on classifying and clarifying stable characteristics of human psychology.

2.  This meaning focuses on the qualities that make people similar. It also pays close attention to human characteristics that differentiate them from other species. It pushes theorists of personality to look into the irregularities in humans that define man's nature and also the elements that influence the course of human life.

These have helped and are still helping to study human personality. Since it is not a one-sided research pattern, the first definition shows that it is a study to determine the very specific qualities that people have. The second definition refers to it as the search for the organized absoluteness of our psychological functions and the relationship between psychological and organic occurrences in people as well as the environment around them.

The two definitions of personality are intertwined; it is however important to note that no definition of personality has been accepted universally within the field of psychology.

Studying personality started with the idea that people are different based on the particular ways that people walk or talk or express how they feel or even arrange their living environment. People who study personality in psychology, called personologists, consider how different people are and how they show self-expression, and then, try to find out why these differences exist.

Even though other parts of psychology study the thinking processes, attention, or motivation, personologists focus on how the different processes come together, mix and help make a distinctive personality.

Systematic study of psychology has driven the study of personality to merge into different study sources. Among them are psychiatric case studies: these studies are more focused on people living with distress. Other sources are the philosophy that deals with man's nature, physiology, social psychology, and anthropology.

## Various Categories of Personalities

Studying personality has been a crucial subject for those interested in psychology. Many theories in psychology have been made over the years, and the major ones have been put into four different categories. These categories referred to as the perspectives of personality try in their own way to outline the various styles in personality. They also describe how these styles are different on individual basis.

### 1. Psychoanalytic Perspective

This perspective focuses on early experiences in individual childhood and how important those experiences are. It also emphasizes on the unconscious mind. Sigmund Freud was the psychiatrist who originated the psychoanalytic perspective. Freud believed that unseen things which were hidden in our minds or our unconscious as he calls it, could be revealed and regained in many ways including slips of the tongue, free association and even through dreams.

Some theorists believed partly in Freud's theory. Neo-Freudian theorists such as Erik Erikson, Carl Jung, Alfred Alder and Karen Horney believed in the importance of the unconscious, but they also did not agree with some other aspects of his theory.

### 2. Human Perspective

The human perspective places the emphasis on individual free will, our personal awareness and psychological growth. The human perspective is more concerned with the positivity of human nature. This perspective also pinpoints how individuals can attain their highest ability.

### 3. Trait Perspective

The trait perspective focuses on pointing out, outlining, and measuring the different traits that form individual personality. When researchers understand these traits that make up individual personality, they will understand better the differences that exist in individuals.

### 4. Social Cognitive Perspective

This personality perspective places its focus on the learning by observation. It is also concerned with the influence of our environment and situations around us and self-reliance as well as the use of cognitive processes.

## Introversion and Extroversion

A once misunderstood personality trait, introversion is now the subject of many discussions, books and articles regarding personality. When many groups of non-scientists began to discuss introversion, a renowned psychologist noticed something. He realized that the way the term introversion was defined by many was contrary to the way he and his colleagues who were academics described it.

The definition of introversion is made from what introversion is not, and that is extroversion. Now, if we say extroverts are bold, self-confident and enthusiastic, people who flourish in highly social environment, then introverts are the exact opposite. That is how academics think of introversion. However, what regular everyday introverts think about the subject or the definition does not match it.

Far back, as early as 1980, was when this problem was identified. At that time, a study revealed that the "common-sense" definitions and the "scientific" definitions were different and did not match. Cheek and his colleagues who included a graduate student, Jennifer Grimes, and Courtney Brown, all continued to think about it. As they also kept interviewing more introverts who were self-described, they were more and more convinced that this already widely accepted definition was less correct.

Cheek now suggests that there is no other way to be an introvert but one. According to him, there are four personality traits associated with introversion. He says that a lot of introverts do not possess just one but a bit of all four traits. These traits are the social, thinking, anxious, the restrained.

Cheek named his model "STAR" (Social – Thinking – Anxious – Restrained). He designed this model by taking the time to survey 500 adults ranging from 18 to 70 years old. He did this survey by asking these people about how much they enjoy spending time alone and in solitude. He also tried to find out how often they daydream.

Here is a brief description of Cheeks' four traits for introversion:

- **Social Introverts**

It can be said that social introversion is the ideal definition of the term introversion. This is because it involves a preference for associating with small groups of people rather than large groups. Social introverts may also prefer to stay alone and not share in any group no matter how small. People who score high in this category may prefer to stay indoors and enjoy solitude.

Social introverts may also prefer to go out in small groups with friends, instead of attending large gatherings and meeting people that they do not know. Although this may be easily associated with shyness, Cheek clearly stated that the social introversion is not the same thing with shyness, since anxiety is the not the driving force for this love for solitude and small groups.

- **Thinking Introverts**

The idea of adding "thinking" as a trait in introversion is a new concept. This group of people, unlike the social introvert, do not hate social events even though it is a general concept to associate introversion with the hate for social events. The thinking introversion refers better to a person who spends time self-reflecting and is more into thoughts. According to Cheek "you're capable of getting lost in an internal fantasy world, but it's not in a neurotic way but rather in an imaginative and creative way".

- **Anxious Trait**

This group is very unlike social introverts; this is because the anxious introverts search for opportunities to be in isolation. This could be because they may feel very self-conscious or even awkward when they find themselves in large groups or just around people simply because they might not be self-assured with their social skills.

In many cases, their anxiety fades away when they find themselves alone and not disturbed with social interaction mostly from people they do not know. This type of introverts usually spend time thinking and contemplating, they keep going over thoughts in their own minds. They tend to overthink about things that have gone wrong, things that are already going wrong and things that can go wrong in the future.

- **Restrained Introverts**

Reserved is another way to render this trait of introversion as a personality. Restrained introverts are a special kind. They prefer not to rush their words or actions, instead they think before talking or acting. If they meet people for the first time, it might take some time before they will loosen up and be free with conversations. They are also a type to wake up and not rush into performing any action. They take their time to carry out their activities.

## How Does an Introvert Behave?

A very popular way that people have described introverts is that they are a category of people who become easily drained just by socializing. They tend to recharge their social batteries by spending time in solitude. The truth is introverts are so much more than just people who enjoy being alone.

At birth, a child is born with a temperament. Temperament refers to the way a person gains energy and how they enjoy relating with the external environment or the world in general. So it can be said that introversion and extroversion are on their own, temperaments.

The genes are what determines if a person will be an introvert or an extrovert and not choice. Which means that people do not get to choose how they turn out, they are born to be extrovert or introvert.

That is not to say that other factors do not affect the process of becoming an extrovert or introvert. People generally are shaped by the things they have experienced in life. If parents and teachers encouraged quiet, thoughtful character in a child, the child will most likely grow up over self-confident.

However, self-confidence may come with a lot of bullying and teasing from others. Peers and relatives may keep telling the individual to be more active with other people by "coming out of their shell". The individual may also develop social anxiety or be forced to pretend to be someone else just so that he or she can fit in.

Indeed, all introverts are not similar. While some introverts might need no time to very little time to recharge their social battery, other introverts might require a longer period to recover from social drainage and recharge.

Some introverts can also handle a reasonable amount of social chit-chat before feeling drained out while others may become drained really quickly. They might also prefer spending longer periods of time alone.

These reactions to social life and events may vary from person to person but most introverts are usually somewhere in between.

Eventually, all introverts will go through, the dreaded phase called the "introvert hangover". This is the phase where an introvert starts to feel like they are totally drained or wiped out as a result for having spent too much time with people. The introvert may be feeling exhausted, may find it difficult to concentrate or may even feel cranky. It may feel like the mental energy in the brain has been used up.

## Most Common Traits of an Introvert

1. Introverts prefer to spend the night at home than to go for social events one after the other.

2. They also enjoy activities that require quiet solitude. They prefer spending time writing or reading, drawing or gardening.

3. Introverts will choose to spend quality time with close friends than having a wild party.

4. Introverts are more productive when they work alone.

5. Many introverts will try their best to avoid any form of social interaction that they regard as unnecessary or small talk.

## Myths about Introversion

It is quite unfortunate that a lot of people do not fully understand what it means to be an introvert. Some think that introversion is shyness while others say it is the same thing as depression and social anxiety. Introverts are usually accused of being stuck up, not interested or angry when they go quiet.

Introverts are also many times accused of having an antisocial or selfish attitude when they decide to spend time alone.

Most introverts know that these statements and accusations are false and misleading. Here is the truth behind such misconceptions that you should know as a mentalist:

1.  Introverts are not really socially awkward people. Shyness and social awkwardness are totally different traits from introversion. Experience has shown that a lot of introverts can be absolutely delightful in social situations.

2.  Contrary to popular opinion, introverts do no despise people or hate them. Many times, introverts may lack the will to have chitchats, and this is usually misinterpreted and seen as a reason to conclude that introverts do not like people.

3.  It is also a misconception that introverts are rude. Lacking social energy can be a trigger for mixed emotions and awkward responses. Introverts can become a bit cranky when their social energy starts getting drained, they could simply zone out during conversations. It will be better to allow them to recharge their social batteries to better interact with them.

4.  Some people also believe that introverts need to be fixed. They do not! It is a part of life and the needs to be understood by all. Being an introvert can be a source of brilliance. Introverts work better when they embrace how they are and channel that energy to give them-selves more strength.

5.  No, extroverts do not wish that they were born with the extroverted traits. It is possible to envy extroverts and their ability for quick thinking and be so socially agile by fitting into almost any social situa-tion. But introverts also enjoy the indoor life and solitude that comes with it, the delight of the inner world of their minds and their alone time.

## Is There Anything Such As A Pure Introvert?

There is not a standard of introversion. There are no two introverts who feel exact same things nor are they exactly alike. A fact for one introvert may be a totally different experience for another introvert. They have differing levels of social tolerance as well as other forms of stimulation.

Carl Jung stated that if a pure introvert existed; "such a man would be in the lunatic asylum". Introversion as well as extroversion have two extremes, they are not traits for all or nothing. This means that at one point or the other, introverts act extroverted and extroverts act introverted. It is not an all or nothing spectrum since the traits are determined by general preference.

## Extroversion and Personality Traits

There is still a lot of things that researchers need to learn with regards to the roots of introversion and extroversion, and so far, a lot of the uncovered information has not been summarized and fed to the public.

However, extroversion can be described as being energized by the external environment. So, if a person is an extrovert, they will often get their energy from going out to meet new people. But here again, not all extroverts are the same. Some are more likely to go out and have more fun than others.

It's important to know how an extrovert behaves. This ensures that you know how to approach them as a mentalist.

There are other definitions of extroversion. For example, extroversion has been broken down into two different sections. They are 'agentic' and 'affiliative' extroversions. Generally, they hold the same principle. Extroverts just want to go out and interact with their external environment.

Depending on the country you live in, extroverts might be called extraverts. However, they mean exactly the same thing.

There is not enough understanding about extroversion. Agentic extroversion is focused on the sensitivity of gains, it also focuses on how individuals deal with their goals and things that they achieve, how they persist and take roles of leadership when the opportunity presents itself.

We can say that agentic extroversion refers to how extrovert individuals deal with the attention brought on themselves or as some may call it, the limelight. The dimension of agentic extroversion is focused on social leadership.

However, affiliative extraversion is more a dimension offering warmth and comfort socially.

People who score high in this trait love to have close relationships with others in their circle, and these social relationships are close to their hearts. Affiliative extroverts benefit a lot from such relationships and usually gain a lot of meaningful friends.

The components of extroversion are just simple ways people enjoy their lives. An interesting fact is that self-reports show that people can score high on both of the components. People can also be high on one while they can be moderate on the other. Even when the traits are matched, a person may still not be the same on both components.

So It can be said that a person who scores very high on affiliative extroversion and scores lower ion agentic extroversion will no doubt have a strong feeling of belonging when they are among friends or even in a religious gathering. However, they might not have the urge to push for a position of leadership.

In a reverse case where the person has a lower score on affiliative extroversion and a higher score on agentic extroversion, it is possible that they will feel a void that needs to be filed, like there is a missing part when they are just hanging around people. This feeling is usually because they want to be among the ones taking the lead.

It can be quite difficult to point out how people feel or will react in different situations. But there is consistency with the prediction that agentic extroversion is focused on getting the reward. The reward in this context could be social, or work related. There is a wide variety of contexts.

Personality traits are related to each other. This means that they are dependent to each other. Personality traits have a normal distribution, meaning that having a very high score on one and a very low score on the other is very unlikely and if at all, very uncommon as scores will be in the middle.

Based on the knowledge of the distribution and the known relationship between both traits, having low scores on both will be just as uncommon as getting high scores on both components.

## The Introvert-Extrovert Spectrum

A lot of things can and have been put into different categories. A good example is the category of right-handed or left-handed people. Eye-color is also categorized. But is it true that everyone falls into the category of introvert or extrovert? Is it true that human personality must either be introverted or extroverted?

A lot of people have the qualities of both introverts and extroverts. Their personalities usually fall between the personality traits. So instead of seeing the personality traits as a label, extroversion can be seen as a spectrum when referring to people who show behaviors that are associated with the two personality traits.

The spectrum of introverts-extroverts is a way to categorize some things in terms of its position between two particular extremes. In this setting, it refers to an individual responding to their environment or situations in a particular pattern.

Consider a bell-curve showing normal distribution with regard to continuous traits, placing extreme extroversion at one end of the spectrum scale and at the other end of the spectrum, extreme introversion. The scale can now account for absolute extroverts, absolute introverts and everyone in between.

The spectrum creates a scale to accurately determine what category individuals fall with regard to their personality traits. It can be easy to proclaim that someone is an extrovert or an introvert, or even an ambivert or omnivert, this conclusion can be based on a personality assessment, however, there are lot of underlining factors including the nature of human behavior, that contribute to making the assessment of human personality traits a broad subject.

## The Ambiverts

Right in the middle of the introvert and extrovert battle, is where ambiverts can be found. This set of people have the energy of introverts and extroverts and can be divided into two categories. The introverted extroverts and the extroverted introverts.

## Introverted Extroverts

Do you sometime feel like you do not exactly fit into the introvert or extrovert groups? Or do you exhibit characteristics of both groups? You just might be an introverted extrovert if you do.

But the guessing pattern is never really accurate. A list of signs has been put together to help people determine if they fall in the group of introverted extroverts or not.

Before diving into the list, it is important to know what an introverted extrovert really is. Who is an introverted extrovert?

A person who is called an introverted extrovert is someone who has high extrovert traits but still displays certain traits of introversion.

Here are some signs of introverted extroverts that you can easily spot as a mentalist:

### Recharge by Meeting People

Introverted extroverts use social interactions as a way to recharge. They recharge by going out to meet new people. Some introverted extroverts also hide in their shells to recharge their social battery.

## Spending Time Alone

Although introverted extroverts get energy from engaging in social interactions, they can also be drained by them. This means that it is deemed appropriate for introverted extroverts to spend long time alone to enjoy solitude after a social event. Looking at it from this angle, being an introverted extrovert is a paradox.

## Passionate Talkative

When introverted extroverts are passionate about a particular subject, they seem to talk a lot about it. An introverted extrovert's world is lit up when a passionate topic is brought up, it might lead to them to talking and expressing themselves very passionately.

## People See You as an Introvert

When people see you or meet you for the first time, they often mistype you as an introvert. This is probably because you are not good with interacting with new people whom your still considers strangers. It is also possible that you feel a bit shy when you meet new people.

# Extroverted Introverts

This is someone who is mainly an introvert but also shows certain traits of an extrovert. For the people who may find it challenging to know if they are extroverted introverts, here are some signs to help you know if you fall under this category of extroverted introvert individuals.

Figuring out who an extroverted introvert can be difficult. Here are few signs to help:

## Carefully Select Conversations

Extroverted introverts try their best to choose the conversations to engage in. They would prefer a conversation that keeps them stimulated, even though they love interacting with others. Extroverted introverts would also be super excited to see that you love the same kind of things that they love.

## Charismatic yet Withdrawn

The first time you meet extroverted Introverts, they always seem very charming and as having charisma. They might seem like they posses all the energy in the world, but as time goes by they just start to withdraw.

## Connection

It is very easy to connect with an extroverted introvert. People find it very easy to connect with them and this is because people love the takes on conversations and how they express them. It is usually the case when wanting to relive the conversation experience with the extroverted introvert.

## Friends

Extroverted introverts have a very tight circle of friends for whom they would do anything. These set of people are separate from the strangers who felt sudden connection and enjoyed just a good conversation.

# The Influence of Personality Differences on Mentalism

Scientists and psychologists as well as other professionals who have contributed in one way or the other to proving the theory of mentalism will be glad to know the extent to which it has grown. The theory is now being put to good use by mentalists around the world, many of which are in the show business.

From time past, mentalists have shown persistence and skill in pulling crowds out of their individual shells. Mentalists have taken over the stage with interesting tricks and a show of mental power over large numbers of people.

They have mastered the art of surprising people with their various stage acts. This is due to the facts that they have taken the time to understand the human brain and find loopholes to how humans reason.

They have also used the sight as a powerful tool in wowing crowds and stealing applauds. Understanding that the human mind is the real reality, they are able to use it to their advantage while performing amazing.

Introverts and extroverts are usually present in places where these shows take place. Some others might have read about mentalism and how it works, while other might be mentalists themselves.

Is mentalism affected by the difference in people personality? The same way it is impossible to accurately tell the level of extroversion or introversion of an individual by just looking at them, it is quite difficult to say how different personalities would be affected on mentalism. So what should a mentalist look out for in people when performing some tricks or trying to read minds? How can he successfully show mind strength and win people over with different personalities?

## What Mentalists Should Look at for When Dealing with People

A good place to start would be understanding the personality of the person. Is he or she an introvert, extrovert or ambivert? Understanding that the introvert is unlikely to want to fully engage in a conversation should help the mentalist vary his tactic by using something more appealing to the introvert. Something relating to solitude and quiet activities that the introvert enjoys. A good example is knowing that the introvert being withdrawn or quiet is not a sign of lying or lack of interest or even guilt.

Extroverts, on the other hand, are more willing to interact with strangers and this is where the mentalist draws his strength. He may need to understand how extroverts think and behave. The mentalist need to understand the "extrovert's advantage" as it would help to get into the mind of the extrovert.

That same technique is required to understand an ambivert. Find out if they are introverted extroverts or extroverted introverts. This will help to get into their minds more easily. To know that the person exhibits characteristics of both introverts and extroverts.

Staying quiet does not mean that an introvert is withholding information and being very chatty does not mean that the extrovert is saying everything that needs to be said. When a mentalist understands this, he or she will tweak their approach to match the personality traits of either an introvert, extrovert or an ambivert.

## How Does It Affect the Behavior of people?

To succeed as a mentalist, you have to know how the personality differences affect the behavior of people in various situations. Here are some areas where our personality differences will have an impact.

### Workplace or Schools

Personality differences can be a problem at the workplace or school. This is because our personalities can not all be the same. The fact that our personalities are not all the same is the reason for many misunderstandings.

But is it an issue if some people are calm when facing life problems while others are totally frantic? Different studies show that our personalities may lead to different outcomes in life. Some of which are morality, our level of education, our status in society, and even our cognitive abilities.

Our personality is closely related to our performance at work. People who get high scores on interpersonal sensitivity, as well as adjustment, are mostly the same ones who are seen as the preferred team members.

But people that get high scores on adjustment and ambition and sociability are those who will be seen as leaders or fit for a position of leadership. The score that individuals get on the personality variable has a significant impact on the possibility of them experiencing certain things in life.

## Health Outcomes

There is evidence to show how personality has a major impact on our health outcomes. A good example is that of Vietnam Veterans when neuroticism and low intelligence predicted how moral they were instead of their age or ethnicity or if they were married or not.

A different study indicates that people who are highly careful, show discretion, and exercise caution are more protected against mortality. People who are well organized or well balanced may live longer than other who are not, and if the person is smart, really old age is more appropriate.

Numerous factors can be responsible for the results or outcomes. We can say that our personality affects how people see health-promoting behavior or even health-harming behavior, and how people are attracted to it.

## Decision-Making

Some people vary when it come to making decisions about how risky their activities will be. People also have various assessment to results or outcomes. A good example is a young man that jumped off the Garden Gate Bridge because of a dare.

## Organization

Our personality also plays a major role in how well our life is organized. People who have low adjustment and a low sense of discretion and carefulness will most likely do less exercise or they will engage in more activities to soothe themselves, such unduly drinking alcohol.

Knowing the effect that the personality traits have on people will allow mentalists to know where to look. They will also be able to ascertain correct understanding of how a person would respond to certain situations.

Generally, mentalists will be able to understand the way people tick. That is really the dream of a mentalist. It's something you should keep in mind.

## Differences between Introverts and Extroverts

Introverts are assumed to be the dichotomous half of the introversion-extroversion personality scope. Introverts are known to be very reflective and private individuals who can be very thoughtful while people know extroverts to be friendly, bold, adaptive, and happy groups of people. They also are more inclined to take risks.

The whole idea of introversion and extroversion is quite a complex and multi-faced personality construct. People can be extreme introverts or extreme extroverts. But people can also be in between the extremes, so they can exhibit both personality traits.

Let us now take a look at a few introvert and extrovert differences in personality about the following:

### 1. Sociability

Extroverts and introverts show very different behaviors when it comes to social situations. Extroverts, for example, show that they prefer to reach out, engage in, and enjoy interacting socially with other people. Introverts, on the other hand, are usually more reserved and shy in social situations. Introverts try to avoid social interactions involving a lot of people.

In 1936, Guilford & Guilford proposed that there are two extremes when it comes to sociability. They were referred to as social dependence and social withdrawal. Some introverts prefer to be quiet and may also enjoy spending time alone and being in solitude while extroverts tend to be more socially available since they make strides on the energy of the people around them. They also usually find themselves as the center of attention when they are in large gatherings.

This does not mean that introverts are anti-social, it just means that they enjoy being away from the simulation of gathering with a large number of people.

## 2. Communication

A postulation, Min Lee & Nass, in 2003 suggested that extroverts' strong social presence is due to thew fact that they talk more and use loud voices. The postulation goes on to suggest that extroverts take-up more physical space by using broad gestures and that they start more conversations with others than introverts do.

While studying a group of students, it was noticed that when they are having conversations with people that they do not know, extroverts gained better eye contact and spoke more than introverts. That study was carried out in 1972 by Rutter, Morley, & Graham.

Generally, extroverts are more confident, and when they interpret nonverbal communication, they interpret them more accurately than introverts (Akert & Panter, 1988).

The art of decoding nonverbal communication by extroverts was termed as "the extrovert advantage". It is believed that extroverts have the skill as a result of their experience in social relationships and their desire to understand people.

## 3. Decision-Making

According to Heaton & Kruglanski in 1991, in situations with time constraints, introverts will most likely make judgments using early information and use those judgments to make decisions a lot faster than extroverts will do.

The research done one the impact of introversion and extroversion about decision-making suggested that extroverts make more quick decisions based on what they feel and it is more natural at that particular moment. It was also found that extroverts show behavior of quality checking before they make decisions.

Researchers also found that extroverts may need someone to direct them when it is time for them to make important decisions. On the other hand, introverts count on themselves and try to avoid making impulsive decisions because they are more thoughtful and intuitive.

## How It Affects People's Actions

1.  Introverts and extroverts respond in different ways to training at their workplace. The study suggested that relaxation training is of more beneficial to introverts than it is to extroverts while ideation skill training may be more beneficial for extroverts than for introverts.

2.  Extroverts prefer to get rewards immediately. They are more sensitive to impulse and display reward-driven behaviors. Extroverts are more likely to get involved in risk-taking activities such as extreme sports.

3.  Introverts and extroverts enjoy different activities. Extroverts participate more in social activities and leisure while introverts prefer activities of solitary leisure.

4.  Another study indicated that extroverts prefer abstract language while introverts are most likely to base their talks on facts.

## Conclusion

Introverts, extroverts and the many other personality types out there is a good study for you in your early mentalist days.

The general aim of learning about people's personality traits is to ensure that you understand the person you will be dealing with as a mentalist.

Of course, just like we said in chapter four, you also have to consider the motivations of the person. Let's talk a bit more about motivations.

# Chapter 7 - The Motivation Factor

## What Motivates People?

Ever thought of what drives people to do the things they do and behave the way they behave? A man was spotted trying to drive through a rocky road. It was very difficult for him because the road was full of obstacles. But he did not stop, he continued striving and working through it. Each time he met a bump he doubled his efforts.

There must have been a factor or a force propelling this man to go further regardless of how uncomfortable the situation was. This factor is his motivation from which he drives courage and willpower.

Motivation comes from the word 'motive'. Motive means desire, needs, or wants that are born in an individual. It is a process of instigating individuals to achieve the desired goal. Simply put, it is the force that fuels all human actions.

Motivation is not all about activating a behavior, it also involves directing and maintaining such behaviors. However, most times, it is difficult to observe such motivations needed to direct and to maintain. That is why mentalists often just make inferences based on observable actions.

Psychologists all over the world have put forward different theories in an attempt to explain the reasons behind our actions. Some of these theories include instinct theory, drive theory, humanistic theory, and

Maslow's hierarchy of needs. The reality is that there are so many things that could compel one to act in a certain kind or to maintain a certain kind of behavior.

There are so many of these forces that you can't put a number on them.

## Types of Motivation

The two main types of motivation often described are intrinsic and extrinsic motivation.

### Intrinsic Motivation

They are the types of motivation that are innate in an individual. They emanate from within an individual. Such motivations include fixing a complex crossword puzzle just for self-gratification or finding the solution to a problem.

### Extrinsic Motivation

This other type of motivation is a result of external factors. They are acquired and not innate. Extrinsic motivation often involves rewards such as money, social recognition, praise, or trophies.

## Importance of Motivation

There are different reasons why people need to remain motivated. In most cases, these reasons are very similar for most human beings. Some of these reasons include:

- Motivation encourages people to take actions
- When motivated, people tend to adopt health-oriented behaviors
- It helps in the elimination of maladaptive behavior and unhealthy habits.
- It helps to promote output in various places of work.

- It makes people feel competent and more in charge of their lives,
- Being motivated promotes happiness and overall well-being.

## Components of Motivation

Motivation is made up of three components and they will be briefly explained below.

### Activation

This is the first component of motivation. Activation is the initial choice or decision to initiate a process. For instance, making up your mind to start taking psychology classes is activation.

### Persistence

The second is persistence. It has to do with commitment and endurance, to achieve your goal even though the road to it doesn't seem so smooth. When you walk through obstacles in an attempt to reach the desired destination, you are said to be persistent. For instance, you keep taking psychology classes to obtain a degree even though some factors make this very difficult. Such factors could include lack of resources, lack of time, or lack of energy.

### Intensity

Intensity is the force or the amount of effort you put into achieving a goal. For instance, student A merely goes to class and takes exams without extra study or stress. On the other hand, not only does student B go to classes, she studies frequently at home, engages in group discussion, and conducts extra research. At the end of the day, student B is more likely to achieve her educational goal while student A will not because she lacks the required intensity.

The amount of attention you pay to each of these components of motivation will determine if you will achieve your goal or not. Strong activation means that your chances of starting to pursue your goal are high. The degree of persistence and intensity will determine if a person will remain in the pursuit of this goal and how long it will take to achieve it.

## Remaining Motivated

Motivation is an essential ingredient in our everyday lives. It is what drives us and keeps us in existence. Without motivation, the advancement in sciences and in arts that we enjoy today wouldn't have been possible. Hence it is very important that we remain motivated.

Remaining motivated might seem pretty difficult at some point in our lives. Because one thing or the other might cause us to lose motivation. When this happens, we become confused and clueless. The good news is whenever you feel in the blues and not motivated, there are a couple of things you could do to get you right back on track.

They include:

- Making adjustments to ensure that the most important things are prioritized.
- If you feel that you are on a project that is too much or too overwhelming for you, try breaking it down into bits. Splitting your goal into smaller tasks will increase your chances of achieving them.
- Work on your self-confidence and make sure it is high enough at all times.
- Remind yourself of your strengths and why you started in the first place.
- Work on your insecurities, keep learning, and acquire more skills to feel more competent.

## Maslow's hierarchy of needs

This is a psychological theory proposed by Abraham Maslow in 1943. Maslow's hierarchy of needs is represented with a pyramid. This pyramid contains the most essential needs of man at the top and going all the way down, the less essential needs in their order of decreasing importance.

This hierarchy of needs serves as a base to study the intrinsic motivation of man that leads to a certain behavior. Maslow used the terminologies "physiological", "safety", "belonging and love", "social", and "self-actualization" to describe the pattern of man-actualization.

According to his explanations, before a man moves to the next hierarchy of need, he must have satisfied the previous stage. The motivation to begin at the next stage only comes when the previous stage has been fulfilled. For instance, a man must satisfy his physiological needs which is the most basic need before moving on to satisfy his safety needs. The ultimate goal is to attain the highest goal which is self-actualization. At this level, the person is completely fulfilled.

## Physiological Need

These are physiological needs essential for the survival of humans. It would be impossible to sustain life without these needs. If these needs are not met, it could lead to discomfort, resentments, and lack of motivation to move on to the next level. Examples of these needs include food, sleep, water, air, clothes, health, shelter, and sex.

## Safety Needs

Once a person has achieved the physiological needs, the person gets motivated to move to the safety needs. Safety needs, as the name suggests, manifest in the need to feel safe. To be protected against natural disasters, wars, childhood abuse, and family violence.

If you don't feel quite safe in an environment, you won't be motivated to love. Safety needs include emotional security, well-being, financial security, and personal security.

## Love Needs

Maslow stated in his explanations that every human has an innate desire to feel a sense of love and belongingness. Regardless of whether the group is big or small, anyone likes to get the feeling to be part of something significant. Love needs include friendship, family, and intimacy. In the absence of these, one might become lonely, anxious, or depressed.

## Esteem Needs

This is the need to achieve stable esteem. These esteem needs were explained in two variations. The lower version consists of the need to be respected by others. The need to be recognized, famous and prestigious. On the other hand, the higher variation includes the need for self-respect, self-confidence, and self-discipline. It also includes the need for mastery, strength, or competence.

## Self-Actualization

Self-actualization lies in the highest level on Maslow's pyramid. This level entails the maximal realization of an individual's potential. According to Maslow, self-actualization is a man's need to achieve everything he can. These needs are usually different for one another. Some people want to succeed athletically, to become a great parent or to create arts better than what has ever existed.

To get to this level, other levels of needs must be satisfied. Self-actualization is regarded as the ultimate goal while other goals are steps that will help you achieve this ultimate goal.

# Factors That Determines the Motivation of a Person

## Promotion

If you desire to get promoted at school or at work, it drives you to put in more effort. Promotion here is the motivating factor and it is external to the individual.

## Achieving a Goal as a Team

Being part of a team gives people a sense of belonging and somehow they want to keep it together. They love seeing their team achieve greater heights and they get motivated by this.

When this sort of people are continually given an increasing milestone, they tend to work harder. Not just for themselves but for the team. They do more generally because team success mean a lot to them.

## Completing a Task

Some people are motivated by the need to complete what they have started. It might be something serious such as a major project or it might be less serious such as a domestic chore. To keep such a person motivated, all you need to do is assign tasks to them and they will be fueled by the need to get the job done.

## Meeting a Deadline

For some people, motivation sets in only when a deadline is closing in on them. With a deadline around the corner, goals look more defined making it easier for them to focus more or better. They can work nonstop until the last minute just to ensure they meet up with a deadline.

Next time you want a job done, set up a deadline and you are bound to get quicker results. Deadlines trigger a sort of motivation in people. With a deadline in sight you get a clearer view of what really matters and the less important things lose more their importance.

## Recognition

Some people are motivated by the need to feel recognized. They might seek this recognition through their families or their place of work. If you give them the slightest idea that their efforts are being recognized, they will work even harder. They work to outshine others in hope that they would get all the more appreciated.

## Security

Human beings have an innate desire to feel secure as a person. Security is one of the basic needs of man. Psychologists believe that only men with a sense of security desire self-actualization.

Hence, the need to feel secured can motivate a person into achieving a desired goal. For instance a man builds a house in order to provide warmth and security for his family. He was able to attain his goal (build a house) because he was motivated by the need to provide security for his family.

## Lifestyle

Some people are driven by the kind of lifestyle they want to live. It could be termed selfishness but not in a negative sense. They want to have a better life or a fancier life so they work hard to achieve that. Their goals are concrete and clearly stated.

For such people, the need to attain a healthier lifestyle keeps them going. If a person is driven by lifestyle, motivating them is only a question of understanding what their end goal is.

## Competition

This is a little bit more like opposition. Creating a competitive environment within a team can make members of such team perform better. Competition in this instance is not about being combative, it's about being productive.

They compete to win and here, competition serves as the factor that influences motivation. The more the competition, the more the motivation and motivation becomes less when the competition is less intense.

## Control

The need to be in control can make people behave in a certain way or engage in certain actions. The need to control time, space and industry can be a force driving an individual to success. Hence, you can initiate a certain action in a person just by giving them control or telling them what to do to attain control.

## Power and Fame

This is one of the most popular factors that drive people. It is not uncommon to hear comments like "I want to become wealthy so that one day I will run for presidency".

While some believe that working hard in pursuit for fame isn't a noble thing, others believe that there can be nothing nobler. If you are in a position to get rewarded with fame or power when you have achieved a goal, you will be compelled to work more.

## Proving Others Wrong

The need to prove others wrong ignites a certain kind of fire in a person. Take for instance a person telling you that you are worthless and can never amount to something. This can act as a source of motivation.

You step out of your comfort zone and do things you might not have done ordinarily just to prove your worth. Barbara Corcoran is a typical example of a lady who was motivated to succeed because she wanted to prove her boyfriend wrong.

## Helping others

Some people drive joy in serving others and this could be a source of motivation for them too. Rendering services to others can be in form of devoting your time and energy or contributing financially to their well-being. Philanthropists fall under this group. They are motivated to do more when they see that in one way or the other, their actions can make the lives of others better.

## Opposition

This is a bit unconventional but some people need an opposition in other to be at their best. This is often obtainable amongst professional performers. They can only be motivated to do more and achieve more if they sense an opposition in the environment/picture.

## The Need to Avoid Embarrassment

Failure comes with embarrassment and shame, and nobody wants to face that. A person who practices a performance severally before acting wants to succeed to avoid being embarrassed.

## Mastery

Being motivated to attain mastery is a little bit different from being motivated to gain control. Mastery is about being a pro in all aspects of a subject. Being a master demands that you know the history, the techniques and all the technology that there is to know in a specific subject.

Mastery requires a lot of practice, time and a defined routine. Most people would willingly turn down the idea of becoming masters in a field because of the high level of commitment it requires. However, some people desire to become masters even though it means very busy schedule and practically no self-time.

## Be the Best (break records)

The thought of shattering records previously made by another person can cause a person to become more enthusiastic. People that are motivated by this factor want their name on top of every list.

They want to be the center of attraction whenever they walk into a room. They don't care about how difficult achieving their dream is. Such people are so driven and they wouldn't stop at anything until they get ahead of everyone else. Anything bigger than them triggers them.

## Make History

Some people are motivated because they want to be remembered when they are gone. They want to be part of history and have their stories told long after they are gone. They are not particularly interested in acquiring wealth although they appreciate it. Their major drive comes from the fact that they want to build a legacy and leave a lasting mark when they are no longer here.

## Enlightenment

Becoming enlightened broadens your knowledge and helps you analyze situations better. An enlightened individual is interested in gathering as much information as possible. Although this is a very uncommon factor, it can still be obtainable for some people. Educationists and professors fall under this group of people. They conduct research and gather information to enable them to make better choices.

## Motivation and Mentalism: How Knowing a Person's Core Desire Can Help You Figure out the Message They are passing

Popular beliefs have it that a mentalist has the ability to read people's mind and say what a person is thinking at a particular point. This is true to an extent. Mentalists demonstrate well developed intuitive abilities.

But the thing most people fail to acknowledge is that mentalists are not spiritualists.

To make a correct guess of what an audience is thinking, the mentalist needs a proper examination of his audience's motives. Motivations are the reason behind every action. Knowing what motivates a person and what his or her core desires are will help you decipher the message they are communicating.

For instance, if you know a student is motivated because she needs a scholarship, it will help you understand why she needs to read and work. Same goes for a man whose need to prove others wrong motivates him. He makes plans to help himself achieve a goal, implements these plans, and evaluates them to ascertain how well he would be able to achieve his goals.

Basically, mentalists perform their tricks using a calculated inference from their audience behavior. Here is another instance. If a mentalist knows that a child is crying because he needs food, he will understand what message the child is trying to communicate with his tears or cries.

## Conclusion

Motivation is the driving force of an individual which can either be intrinsic or extrinsic. The best mentalist is one who can interpret his audience's behavior based on the perceived motive behind such behavior. Therefore, he must understand what motivation is and the factors that can influence said motivation.

# Chapter Eight - Mentalist Tricks to Help you Read and Analyze People Effectively

————

Have you ever sat down and thought about how it would feel like to be able to correctly guess and analyze what the person next to you may be thinking? Sometimes, you meet people who tend to employ the use of their intuitions to achieve this. But what if like many, you're not gifted with the ability to perceive people's personalities as fast as possible? It simply means that you need to learn and master the "hows" of reading and analyzing people effectively.

About 55 percent of the information we are given access to are formed via the help of non-verbal methods of communication. Everyone you meet has a way of expressing their thoughts and feelings through either their gestures, mimics, or certain body language.

When you learn how to study and read people, there's a high possibility of you developing a good human relationship with them. Simply put, the ability to analyze people enhances effective communication between you and others.

Now, what are the specific things to pay attention to? What tricks should you apply to figure out the different signs that give a hint of what someone else's thoughts are? These, and more, are what we shall take a look at in this chapter:

## Body Language - What it means

As the name suggests, body language refers to different types of non-verbal communication involving physical conduct rather than words, as a way of expressing or passing Information across one or multiple persons. Some of this physical behaviors are:

- Touch

- Eye movements

- Body positions

- Face expressions

- Body gestures

- Space, etc.

Otherwise known as kinesics, body language isn't only seen in human beings, it is also displayed by animals and all living things alike. Even though it's an essential part of communicating, many of the non-verbal communication by human beings is often done subconsciously.

Moving on, this form of communication (body language) isn't the same thing as sign language. This is because unlike it, sign language fully functions like spoken languages; it comes with grammatical structure and also features properties just like every other language you know. But in the case of body language, there's no grammar structure attached to it nor does it have specific meanings; most body languages can be interpreted correctly based on context.

## What are the Mentalist tricks that help you read and analyze people effectively?

The truth is, you don't have to be a questioner to find out what the next person may be thinking in their head. Why? Because there are always pronounced or subtle signs that easily give these thoughts away. Here are some of the tricks that some mentalists have employed in recent times, to help them read minds as effectively as they could:

## 1. The Biting or Chewing on their Glasses' Arm

Usually, people tend to firmly place objects or items against their lips when they are trying to make a huge decision. It can also serve as a form of reassurance.

Most people who wear glasses are seen time and time again, practicing the "glasses-arm-in-mouth gesture". This is the act of sucking on the arms or frames of one's glasses. It's a nonverbal form of communication that most times means that a person's mind is buried with deep thoughts. This is also the same for people who either chew on their fingernails, pens, etc.

Do you have a friend or an acquaintance who wouldn't let their teeth off their glasses? If yes, then the best thing to do at this point is to be a support system for them. This is because a lot of the time, the glasses-arm-in-mouth gesture is done subconsciously, so it can easily pass as a sign of deep worry. Like breasts, sucking on the arm of glasses may provide one with a sense of security or feeling of safety.

## 2. Closing the Eyes

Closing the eyes is a simple gesture that's commonly found in philosophers. When someone keeps closing their eyes while speaking, this could be an indicator that they are trying to connect directly with their internal feelings. This feeling may be physical, or emotional. Closing your eyes while speaking is a way of going inside and connecting with your feelings, whether they are physical things or emotional. It is a 'posture' or gesture commonly found in philosophers.

Just like the gesture implies, closing the eyes is also a way of shutting out the rest of the word. People who often do this are trying to tell the next person that they do not like what they see and will love to be left alone. It's also a way of trying to avoid direct eye contact with whoever may be sitting opposite them during a conversation. In this case, any further efforts to get the person to look at you may become a total waste.

Note, while communicating with visual thinkers, you may observe their fondness for closing and opening their eyes at intervals. This is their way of creating images in their head without interruption from the outside world. It's important to understand that if someone is speaking to you and keeps closing their eyes, they are trying to be isolated from the world you see.

Again, a person closing their eyes while in a conversation with you doesn't mean that they are scared to talk to or with you. Different from that, it often means that they are fed up and would want you to leave their sight. So what should you do when you see someone closing their eyes while in a discussion? Run!

In the end, closing-the-eye can be interpreted as a lot of things - impatience, imagination, irritation, etc., as though the person is trying to come to terms with their current thoughts at the time they're with you.


## 3. Hand-Rubbing

One body language that's frequently seen in our everyday life is the hand-rubbing gesture. It is said that when people rub their hands, it could mean that they are anticipating something or enjoying the sight of something that's placed before them.

For example, your mum promised you your favorite meal as a reward for something great you did. Now, subconsciously, you may rub your hands together for a while. Rubbing of hands in this context simply means that you're having high expectations as well as anticipating the cooking of the said meal. When she finally makes the meal and serves you, you will most likely rub your hands again alongside an almost silent "mmm" to show that you love what's before you (the food).

In some other cases, people use hand-rubbing gestures to show how stressed they are at a given moment, and also how positive they are about something coming forth to relieve them of the stress. Since the hands directly or indirectly project certain thoughts we have in our heads, rubbing hands together sometimes signifies the feeling of hope - something beneficial to come in the future.

## Hand-Rubbing Speed

Depending on the speed, hand-rubbing can mean different things.

If one is rubbing their hands quickly, it means that they are feeling highly positive about themselves. But when the hand-rubbing is going at a slower pace, it may signify that the person is thinking of a plan that would hurt someone else. This is specifically shown in most cartoons or movie villains. There's also a case of one hand-rubbing with interlaced fingers - this means that they are having doubts about something.

When dealing with people, especially in a business transaction, you should always look out for the hand-rubbing gesture; people use it to show when they are comfortable or uncomfortable about the conditions or terms of negotiation you're offering them.

## 4. Clasping or Squeezing of Hands

You must have noticed people fix and squeeze their hands into each other. This is because at that time, the person could either be going through an anxiety phase, feeling scared, or uncomfortable, hence the reason for the hand clasping gesture. Doing this helps them to reassure themselves that everything will be fine.

Regarding hand clasping, there are different variations, and each of them tends to pass distinct meanings across. Some of these variations are:

## Handclasp with Intertwined Fingers

This indicates that a person is frustrated or having disturbed thoughts about a situation, so they do this to keep their emotions in check. This gesture is also seen in people who are undergoing some form of routinization which may include:

- Live TV interview
- Being the center of attraction in a gathering

## Palm-to-palm handclasp

In this case, one of the palm is usually placed on the other. It's almost the same thing as joining hands with someone else, which comes with gentle rubbing. This further indicates that anyone who is seen practicing the palm-to-palm handclasp gesture is simply searching for a sense of safety or security - it provides maximum comfort to the mind.

Furthermore, a lot of people think of this as the best human body gesture that offers relief to the mind. Highly supportive people are known to do this more often than not. Palm-to-palm handclasp is most common in these categories of people:

- People who are going through financial distress
- A person who has suffered severe criticism
- A sick patient in the hospital's waiting room

## Fingers in Palm Handclasp

This variation of hand clasping deals with the top and bottom hand. The palm, alongside the fingers of one hand (the upper hand), is wrapped around the fingers of the second hand (the bottom hand). Unlike the other types, the Fingers in Palm hand clasping isn't as comforting.

If you find anyone who's practicing this gesture, it means that they aren't feeling so insecure. Rather, they are putting it up as an "act" performed to portray them as respectable beings. This version of handclasp isn't seen all the time but can be witnessed in specific places and gatherings such as:

- Wedding ceremonies
- Charity events
- High valued seats at sporting events

Generally, hand clasping occurs when someone is seated. This way, their hands are placed on their lap or on a table. The lap and the table are the most regular surfaces where hands are clasped on, and it's a way of showing that one is mildly insecure at the moment. Hands-on the torso, and the elbows rightly held to the sides, are other means of hands clasping. Doing it in this position enables one to be more comfortable as the torso provides pressures which in turn, feels like a hug.

Also, if hands are positioned in front of one's throat while keeping their arms in contact with the front of their body, this signifies a high level of stress. Observations show that the throat is one of the most vulnerable parts of the body, so if one is trying to protect it, then it means they are going through a difficult phase. Someone can decide to touch themselves with their arms as it provides the body with a relieving feeling.

## 5. Hand on the Mouth

Hand on the mouth is a subconscious gesture that often occurs as soon as the brain instructs it to do so. It's usually an indication that one is about to conceal misleading or unplanned words that they or the next person has said. The hand on mouth gesture takes two variations which are:

- Multiple fingers on the mouth
- A closed/clenched fist over the mouth

However it may occur, this gesture always conveys the same meaning. Everyone who had a good childhood had at one point in time, displayed this gesture, either as a way of preventing themselves from saying something, or a means of stopping saliva-splash during cough. Even in adulthood, a fist, fingers, plan over the mouth is a means of suppressing unwarranted words from flowing out. But in a situation when someone accidently lets out unintended, inappropriate words, they can also place their hands over their mouth to show how sorry they are, and would love to take back their words to stop further damaging words from flowing.

In addition, covering the mouth with hands is a known way of showing that one is shocked or surprised at something they saw or heard at a particular time.

Let's picture Gabriel, an 8-year-old boy who asked his parents to purchase a brand new bicycle for him. Realizing that his parents have always complained about not having enough money, he places his hands over his mouth, indicating how sorry he is to have requested this in the first place. He goes about his life, sad, but making up his mind to forget everything about owning a bicycle anytime soon. One day, Gab's parents call him into their room and point in the direction of the window which reveals a bicycle parked outside the compound. On seeing the bicycle, he puts a hand over his mouth, places the second one, and gives out a smile.

From the above scenario, you can see that the significance of the hand on the mouth gesture is duly represented. The next time you see anyone displaying this gesture, do well to pay attention and find out what they could be thinking at the period of display.

## 6. Facial Expressions

Sometimes, the expressions on our faces can help to tell the next person what we feel about a situation on hand. Someone may tell you that they aren't lying, but because they are wearing facial expressions that say otherwise, you can be able to tell that they are lying - not as fine as they want to make it seem. Some of the emotions that can be conveyed through facial features or expressions include but are not limited to:

• Disgust

• Happiness

• Desire

• Enjoyment

• Fear

• Surprise

• Sadness

• Contempt

• Anger

• Excitement

When discussing with someone, it's important that you pay attention to their face, as it helps you tell whether they believe and trust your words or not. For instance, slightly raised eyebrows and soft smiles suggest that a person is confident and comfortable when they're with you, and would love to be friends too.

Furthermore, facial expressions such as hands-on the chin, are used by most people of the opposite to attract someone they truly like. Hands-on the chin gesture signifies; "hey, here I am, you can take and do as you wish with me". It's advised that everyone takes note of this and then decides if the gesture is worth reciprocating or not.

**How to Spot Facial Expressions**

It's one thing to understand that human beings give out different expressions with their faces to convey meaning, it's another to understand how to read them. The following describes how to spot and tell what one could be thinking through their facial expressions:

**Small expressions**

These expressions do not stay on the face for a long time. If you are a regular observer, you may not be able to see them as they come and go as quickly as they can. You should, however, pay more attention to someone especially if you already have a sort of feeling about their persona. This way, you don't miss out on the simple, important details.

**The Eyebrows**

The next thing to take note of is the eyebrows. This is because a lot of the things people think about are expressed through them. Eyebrows and what they depict include:

- Drawn up inner corners - sadness
- Raised and arched - shocked, surprised
- Turned down and joined together - anger

**The Eyes**

Following the eyebrows, is the eyes. They tell an in-depth meaning of an expression more than the eyebrows do. The different depictions of the eye expressions can be:

- Intense stare - anger
- Widely opened - surprised
- Wrinkled on the sides of the eye - happy
- Dilated pupils - romantic interest, fear
- Rapid blinks - stressed, dishonesty

**The Mouth**

This is the last facial piece that helps to pass meaningful expressions across. You should always look out for:

- Widely opened mouth - fear, scared
- Jaw drop - surprised, astonished
- Mouth raised on one side - hate
- Mouth raised on the corners - happiness
- Corners of the mouth drawn down - sad

To get used to the different emotions that people communicate through their faces, you can start practicing them. Doing this helps you to improve on recognizing them faster.

## 7. Holding or Propping the Chin

Since the head is quite heavy, a lot of people subconsciously support it by holding it up with their hands. When someone is seen propping their chin, it may be a slight indication that they are having deep thoughts about something. If you just made an offer to someone and they go on to hold their chin, then it means they are trying to evaluate or judge your offer, to see if they will be making the right or wrong decision to accept it.

Besides, boredom is a reason why most people, especially men, hold up their chin. Boredom can cause you to sleep so to avoid being utterly embarrassed, a handheld to your chin can prevent your head from dropping. Observations have proven that chin propping is a behavior that's common with good listeners – it shows that one is raptly interested in whatever you have to say to them.

Equally, signals can be communicated using the chin propping gesture. Examples of this can be seen when one is agreeing or disagreeing through a nod.

Other reasons why people hold their chin include:

**For Protection**

This is most especially seen during fights. Since the chin is one of the most vulnerable parts of the human body, people protect it at all costs and their prey wouldn't gain direct hit at it. What's more, propping the chin does not only protect it, but it also shields the throat which is even at a bigger risk, from getting a share in the hurt. This means that in some situations, holding the chin is undoubtedly a defensive measure that most people take whenever they feel insecure or threatened.

**To Prove Loyalty**

Propping the chin can sometimes serve as proof of one's loyalty to another. During this act, the head is slightly tilted down or to the side, with the eyes looking somewhat downcast. Shy people, as well as people in romantic relationships, express this a lot.

## 8. False Adjusting of Tie

This act is mostly performed when there's a trace of discomfort, anxiety, fear, worth, concern, and vulnerability in a person. For women, it could be mere fondling of the necklace. If the person in question is a leader, it's easier to conclude that they are feeling uneasy at the time of this subconscious act.

Again, this gesture depicts different meanings; it all depends on the situation. An instance can be seen in a man or a woman who is near someone of the opposing sex for whom they show attraction to. In this case, it means they are attracted to them and maybe feeling nervous or uncomfortable about their current situation.

## 9. Crossed Arms

The crossed arm gesture is easily one of the most common body language that will help you analyze a person's thoughts within a short time. When someone crosses their arms, the different perceptions may include:

- Insecure
- Resistance
- Anxious
- Tensed
- Afraid
- Response to distress

Usually, there are times when people feel overwhelmed and stressed and would want to find comfort and relief in themselves. When this is the case, crossing tightly the arms can be a means for them to effectively mark their boundaries, in a bid to prevent other people from getting through to them.

It's no surprise that most people are comfortable when in the crossed arm positions. Why? Because it helps them to shuffle off from the rest of the world. Simply put, it's also a way of showing someone's irritation towards a thing.

Because the crossed arms gesture comes with different interpretations, you may need to focus and analyze contexts to reach a clear understanding. For instance, if you're in a discussion and the person you're talking with is seated with their arms crossed, and their eye fixed directly at you, this can mean that their mind is fully present and they are listening with rapt attention to whatever you are saying.

## 10. Feet Positions

Other than being used for locomotive purposes, feet positions are part of the body gestures that most people have failed to take notice of. Analyzing and reading people can be much easier if some of these positions are understood. This is because the feet tell the truth, and can give away someone's intent in no time.

Like most non-verbal forms of communication, the feet position gestures are quite easy to read and understand. Certain details that can be easily missed are provided through the feet gestures. If you are looking to know when someone is fully interested in having a conversation with you or to know when to approach your favorite person at a public meeting, then it's advised that you pay further attention to the position of their feet.

Depending on the position of one's feet, emotions such as joy, worry, fear, confusion, can be detected.

The different feet position gestures to master include:

### Feet on the Table

In an office setting, one putting his feet on the table always may be subtle evidence that he or she is the boss. This is usually seen during a meeting or a gathering, and they are trying to let the others know that it is a proper conversation. This way, everyone is aware of their environment and would know better than not to act accordingly. A leader hanging his feet on the table also means that they are:

- Curious about something
- Vulnerable
- Trying to bridge a distance
- Transparent
- Original/authentic, etc.

Asides from being bossy, the feet on the table gesture can help to prove that one is impolite, disrespectful, and has little to no regard for the people around. Some psychologists are of the opinion that anyone who feels great about being in this position should rather do it in private, maybe at home.

## Feet Pointing Forward

If the feet are pointed towards you, then it's a simple indication that the person has an interest in you. It's one of the fastest ways to easily spot the intention of someone without them knowing. Most times in a large gathering, people tend to point their feet towards the speaker or the most charming person in the room.

## Feet Pointing Away

Think back to the times that you've lost interest in certain conversations, you'd notice that you had your feet pointed away, possibly towards the exit or any other easy direction of escape. Almost everyone has been there. This gesture can also apply to other human beings.

If someone is pointing in another direction, then you should know that the person wants to withdraw from where they're standing or sitting. In other words, they have less interest in you.

## Dangling/Swinging Shoe

This gesture is commonly seen in women, where they reveal the heels of their shoes. If a woman does this while on a date with you, do not think too hard as this may mean they are highly interested in you as well as feel comfortable talking with you. It's also a way to show that one is playful, excited, or even flirty.

## 11. Body Posture

Posture is another means of showing what one is thinking as well as one persona. To know if someone is open, confident, or submissive, you can decide to pay a closer look at their posture. For example, someone sitting upright signifies that they are focused. Whereas sitting with a hunched-forward back means boredom or feeling indifferent about the current situation.

In reading or analyzing people, look out for their posture as they are capable of sending meaningful signals across. The two common body postures we have are open and closed postures.

## Open Posture

When in this position, the body trunk is kept open in a bid to expose it. Anyone who does this is either open, friendly or simply marking their willingness to do something.

## Closed Posture

This is the opposite of the open posture. Here, the trunk of the body gets hidden by hunching the upper part of the body forward. The arms and legs are also kept crossed here. This posture indicates anxiety, hostility, or unfriendliness.

## 12. Leaning Forward

When people are nursing positive attitudes towards others, leaning froward gestures are subconsciously practiced. In other words, this gesture is meant for people who genuinely love and enjoy each other's company. Verbal communications also improve when both parties are involved.

This gesture isn't planned as it naturally comes as long as there's a form of likeness existing between individuals. The legs stay entirely motionless in this position, while the body leans forward spontaneously. Leaning forward to you goes to prove that they have interests in you, your ideas, or anything you have to contribute.

In addition, most business meetings require the leaning forward gesture. This way, the presenter is given an assurance that the attendees are fully participating in the event.

## 13. Leaning Back

This is the exact opposite of the leaning forward gesture. Here, people show how tired they are about a conversation by pulling their body in the backward position. This may be because of how uncomfortable they feel concerning the person at the other end. If someone displays this gesture towards you, it's safe to say they are displaying negative attitudes as a result of dislike or hate.

Again, this a subconscious act that's often triggered by dangerous or unpleasant scenarios. It's also a way of showing dominance over people or objects.

## 14. Eye Contact

Like what a window is to a house, the house is inarguably the quickest way to see through one's mind. This is because it makes way for easy communication. Through the eyes, the emotions and feelings of others can be read and analyzed. Most lovers, for example, fix their gaze on each other's eyes, hoping to read their minds through the pupils. This is made possible through the enlargement of the pupils. When one is angry, it's easy to tell as their pupil begins to reduce in size.

For a lot of people, the visual senses are the most dominant. This is why making eye contact with people is one of the most essential forms of non-verbal communication. Through eye contacts, you can detect when someone is going through the following emotions:

- Affection
- Attraction
- Interest
- Hostility
- Happy
- Discomfort

Lastly, gauging the involvement of other people in a discussion can be quite easier if you're able to analyze them through their eyes.

## 15. Crossed Legs

The way people cross their legs can give away the particular emotion that they may be feeling at a specific point in time.

### Ankle Crossing

One crossing their legs at the ankle may prove that they are trying to conceal something.

### Knee Crossing

The most popular term used to describe this leg crossing posture is the "four-figure" position. If the legs are crossed at the knee and pointing away, it shows that one is uncomfortable with whomever they may be talking with. The next indication of the four-figure posture is that one is powerful, confident, approachable, or even exerts authority.

## Other Mind Reading Tricks

The following are some other tricks that can help you as a Mentalist to effectively read people's minds:

### 1. Twisting or Twirling Your Hair

If you watch lots of movies or TV shows, you must have noticed that this gesture is commonly used to depict a flirtatious woman. This is mostly accompanied by the look they give through their eyelashes. In reality, it's said that people who are feeling uncomfortable or nervous about a situation, either twists their hair as a method of keeping the mind relaxed. Women also twirl their hair either as a hint of their Innocence, absent-mindedness, or tiredness.

However, some hair-twirling acts occur as a result of insecurity or worry. A person who does this should be monitored at a close range to prevent severe psychological problems from happening. Other than that, there are no significant consequences attached to the twirling of hair, since it's a subconscious act that most women are used to.

## 2. Nails Biting

A lot of kids and teens alike grow up biting their nails and never grow out of this habit. If you find an adult who bites their nails, chances are that they started it when they were much younger and then found it hard to stop. The nail-biting body language shows when one is nervous or insecure. It also signifies that one is going through some mental or emotional distress. If you're speaking to them at the time of the nail-biting, it may be a slight indication that you're getting them nervous. This can be good or bad; it all depends on the situation.

Since nail biting is usually an unplanned act, boredom and hunger are other reasons why people do it as it serves as a coping mechanism.

## 3. Licking the Lips

As a woman, if a guy does this in a way that seems as though they are moisturizing their dry/chapped lips, then it means that they admire you, there's a chemistry that you two share, and may want to be involved in a romance with you. It also shows that he enjoys your company.

## 4. Looking Downwards

This is a body gesture that's often displayed by people who are less confident in themselves. It comes off as a sign of weakness sometimes. This body gesture is regarded as a bad one and people should try as much as possible to maintain eye contact with whomever they are.

# Factors to Consider When Reading and Analyzing Other People

In either verbal or non-verbal hints, you need to seek certain factors that should be put into considerations. Going just by logic won't reveal all that you want to know. It's about knowing, beyond words, what other people want to say. You must learn how to truly sense what they mean at all times.

Also, the moment you learn how to read people, your personal, social, and work-life tends to develop into something better. This is because understanding how other people are feeling at any given moment allows you to tailor your message better to fit their current mood. To do this, you do not need unique power; you only need to master the techniques. To further elaborate on this, here are some of the factors to consider when reading and analyzing other people.

## 1. Be Objective

Being open-minded is the first step to analyzing people. This means that your previous experiences, emotions, and opinions about people shouldn't come into play while you're on this exercise.

## 2. Form a Baseline

A lot of people are known to come with different unique behavioral patterns. An instance can be someone looking downwards during a conversation, touching their head, rubbing their neck, crossing, their arms, jiggling their feet, etc. You will most likely not notice until you really paid attention to them.

Each behavior displayed by a person is done for specific reasons. It can also just be a mannerism they adopted right from birth. Deception, nervousness, anger, happiness, etc. are indications that may come with each of these behaviors. Forming a mental baseline of every behavior exhibited by human beings will enable you to read people better.

## 3. Seek for Deviations

The next thing to do would be to pay more attention to certain variations in the baseline that you've formed. Variations can occur in their words, the way they sound, or their gestures.

Let's say: you have a friend who nails bites. Paying closer attention, you notice they mostly do this when they are bored or feeling hungry. All of a sudden, they get a job and this gesture starts occurring whenever it's time to leave for work. At this point, you may want to give this habit a different meaning as it now seems to appear as a result of nervousness.

At the end of the day, you can only find out what each gesture truly means when you ask the person relevant questions. This will help you to know the exact cause of the deviations.

## 4. Observe the Clumps of Gestures

Generally, when words and gestures are said or shown alone, they may not convey a perfect meaning at first. However, when there are many clusters of deviations in the behavioral pattern, it's advised that you observe closely.

Assuming your friend who nails bites decides to move from that to twirling her hair? Then not only that, but she has her face looking withdrawn while at it? The next option would be to counsel them appropriately.

## 5. Check for Comparisons and Differences

If someone starts acting a bit differently from what they are used to, and you notice, you may want to enhance your observation. This is to check where and when they exhibit this new behavior(s) with you or other people you know.

The observation should go on for as long as it can, preferably when they talk with other people in the room. What are their facial expressions like? How about their body language? Did anything change? Pay attention to small details.

## 6. Look via the Mirror

The human body is wired in a way that we all have mirror neurons. The mirror neurons can be seen as monitors that are built and planted into our brains to help reflect whatever other people may have in their minds.

There's the smile muscle that gets activated the moment you smile, then there's the frown muscle that activates once you frown, and the list goes on. This is purely evident in some of our daily relationship with other people; when you develop a certain likeness for a person, it shows in ways that:

- Your facial muscles feel relaxed
- The manner with which your head tilts
- The arch in your eyebrows, etc.

When these gestures aren't reciprocated, looking into the "mirror" will help you find out that the other person isn't generally feeling the same way you feel about them.

## 7. Notice the Way They Walk

The way a person walks helps you to understand their persona. For example, one who isn't steady with their leg movements may depict a shy or less confident person. If you ever notice anyone with such habits, praising or commending their efforts once in a while may help strengthen their self-esteem and also steady the way they walk. You also need to act as you believe in the ideas and insights they share.

## 8. Notice the Tone of Their Voice

Strong or weak? One's voice allows you to figure out the kind of person they are. A confident person, for example, will most likely display a comprehensible posture, a wide smile, or a strong voice. Note, being loud doesn't directly translate to one having a strong voice - you will have to study the differences to know.

When you find yourself in a team or group, the team leader may not have a loud voice like the random member of the team. Identifying the tone of one's voice strategically increases your chances of knowing them better.

## 9. Observe Personality Hints

Everyone is born with a personality that's mostly specific to them. Observe and clarify the personality hints and you will be fine in reading and analyzing them correctly.

## 10. know How to Identify Action Words

Words are specifically representative of a person's thoughts and the meanings that may be embedded in them. Simply put, they are the easiest way to get into someone else's head. To identify action words means that you have to be a good listener as it's the only way you will be able to accurately point things out.

# Conclusion

By now, you must have understood that pointing out the struggles of others and understanding how to accommodate them is important. But then, this isn't possible if you're still finding it hard to identify the personality type of the people around you. Having the ability to read is a skill that can enhance your emotional quotient (EQ).

In this chapter, we have addressed some of the important things to note about human behavioral patterns as well as how to use them as a cue to identify personality types.

# Chapter Nine - Top Skills You Must Learn If You Want To Be Successful At Mentalism

————

## Introduction

One important thing worthy of note is that learning mentalism is not a quick and haphazard process. It is just like learning to play guitar. You don't jump right in and start playing different songs. You start by familiarizing yourself with the basics and each individual chord. Once you know your way around these chords, you can now pull them together to start making music.

In mentalism, you don't begin with manipulating the minds of 10 people all at once. You start from basics, just like the chords in a guitar, and over time, you develop competence. Basics here doesn't necessarily mean easy, rather it means important. Even the most basic task in mentalism can prove to be very difficult. These basics form the fundamentals of every effect in mentalism.

Mentalism is a type of art that involves a display of intuitive and mental abilities by performing artists usually referred to as mentalists. During the process of mentalism, the performing artist can employ mediumship, precognition, clairvoyance, hypnosis, divination, mind control, and rapid mathematics.

A mentalist is one who, through a series of techniques, is capable of conjuring an individual's mind in an other to achieve a predetermined outcome. Usually, at first glance, a person would think that mentalism employs psychic or supernatural powers. But in an actual sense, it is a mere twist of the psych.

Mentalism alter reality with explorations of influence, psychology, and suggestion. Most times, mentalists are regarded as psychic entertainers. But the problem here is that psychic entertainers also engage in non-mentalist performances such as psychic reading.

According to Penn & Teller, the major difference between a mentalist and a psychic is that a mentalist is honest and open about the skill he has. He admits to being an entertainer or an artist whose art demands study, natural means, and intensive practice. On the other hand, a psychic believes he has some sort of supernatural and extraordinary power. He carries out his performances in what a mentalist will describe as being unethical.

To excel in any art, dedication, extensive skills and practice are very important. It is also the same in mentalism. You learn gradually, from simple to complex until you become grounded in the art.

## Qualities of a Good Mentalist

All professional mentalists have some traits in common which enable them to excel in their fields. Below are some qualities you must possess if you want to become a good mentalist.

### Understand the true meaning of mentalism

Mentalism is not magic, every mentalist should know this much. In mentalism, the mentalist provides entertainment for his audience by exploring their minds. Although you can be a magician and a mentalist at the same time, these two roles must be properly differentiated. Whether your specialty is in psychology or the psychic field, it all results in the creation of a mentalism experience.

Remember that to fully understand mentalism, you have to practice and perform. Mere theories can't provide in-depth knowledge. Professionalism and financial benefits are not always a factor. You can decide to get into the art just for the fun of it and for general social purposes. Whatever the reasons, you must treat mentalism as a serious business.

## Have a passion for mentalism

One of the strongest factors that drive many professional mentalists is the passion they have for the cause. If you are not sure you love mentalism, don't venture into it. It is not easy to play the role of a mentalist.

There will always be compromises but you will achieve the desired result only when the love and passion is there. You must show genuine interest in the history, the study as well as the performance. You must also be willing to explore, create authentic ideas, and remain creative.

Even though you are not a professional yet, you must act like one. This is the only way your audience will take you seriously. Always be willing to learn more even as you practice. At the end of each performance, make a mental assessment. Take note of the things you did right and take the things that need improvement.

## Have an apparent premise as a performer

A good mentalist has a well-defined premise as a performer. He has a story, a chronicle, a direction, and a destination. If you are to become successful as a mentalist, you should have a start too. A clear definition of who you are as a performer will help you develop concordance. How do you feel reading the minds of others? What do you see, letters or images? What kind of sensations do you get while on stage?

If you have too much trust in your talents, you will end up lazy and unsuccessful. Talent alone doesn't guarantee success. Talent is just one factor, it is not the only factor. To succeed you need more discipline, hard work, and constant efforts in striving for the best. That is the only way you can create significant changes.

Lastly, you need to have a strong belief in your premise. It's not enough to just confess them. You need to believe. Remember, mentalism is closely associated with the philosophical school of thought. In this school of thought, the mind is everything and everything is of the mind. So you will only have it in reality if you have it in the mind.

## Awareness of Potential

To be successful at mentalism, having the potential is not enough, you need to be aware of it. You need to explore the uniqueness of your personality because that is your strength. The keyword here is your uniqueness, you can't explore your uniqueness if you don't even know what it is. Hence you must embark on a consciously self-discovery journey.

When you become fully convinced of who you are, your mentalism will be more authentic and it will reek of realness. You will become more alive on stage and your performances will automatically get better. You can create your routine or adopt that of others.

Many popular mentalists from around the world are known to have keyed into the routine of other people and they still did great. The point is, you don't have to use a routine that you created. As long as it works for you, you are good to go. Some mentalists are not bold enough to come up on stage. But through their unusual techniques, they have contributed immensely to the art and raised the bars significantly.

## Be bold

This is probably one of the most important qualities you have to possess as a mentalist. This was particularly emphasized by the great David Hoy in his philosophy. A performer is considered bold if he or she is confident and communicates his or her message convincingly.

Being bold can be pretty hard. Most times when you try, you end up leaving techniques out of the performance in an attempt to focus on your charisma and personality. As difficult as this might be, it gets better with practice. If you practice well enough, you can use whichever method you want to with confidence.

Boldness is required in carrying out the simplest techniques, it is also required if you are to go all out with your audience. However, you must resist the urge to play the "Mr. Incredible". Experts have proven that the more you put to be incredible, the less incredible you will be.

Be bold enough to take risks no matter how slim the chances of success are. You could be wrong but there is nothing wrong with being wrong so you shouldn't be scared. Sometimes, the wrong move or the wrong guess makes your performance more credible. When you learn to let your intuition flow while taking a calculated risk, you will be surprised at the results you will get.

## Be an interesting person

A good mentalist shouldn't attract attention only on stage, you should be an interesting and fun person even backstage. You should be able to engage in an interesting conversation with a random person you meet on the streets.

Be a good listener and always have a story to tell. You must be able to engage people even without your tricks on stage. This way, you are confident that you can always leave an impression on people and not just entertain them. Your relevance without your tricks proves that you are capable of forming a strong connection with people.

## Have curiosity for various practices and topics

Apart from mentalism, there should be other topics you should show interest for. You will find it surprising that those other topics are the key to your creativity. If you are a fan of music, develop a routine based on songs you like. You can even decide to play one or two instruments while on stage. If you like poetry or science fiction, use one of your favorite poems or books and do a mind-reading.

Explore a lot in other areas you enjoy. Also, try out things that don't quite interest you in the present moment. Meet people, converse with them and show you care. You can tell if a performer is versatile when you watch him perform. A versatile artist can always spice up his show with different themes. The audience appreciates versatility and novelty and they look forward to seeing one in every show.

## Surround yourself with people who inspire you

A good mentalist makes a conscious effort to surround himself with inspiration. If you dream of becoming one, then you should certainly do the same. Discuss your goals and dreams with other mentalists. Learn from other people's performances and take note of corrections when you perform in the presence of other mentalists. Other people's experiences can be a source of motivation to you even though you don't know them.

Tap into such experiences and keep striving to do better. You never grow or do better if you are too comfortable in your current position. Get up, meet people, talk with them and find out what they know. Play the role of a student more than you play the role of a performer. Intrinsically, mentalism is a mind-expanding activity that opens you up to new possibilities. It doesn't quite make a whole lot of sense to be a mentalist without a better self.

## Love your audience

No matter how you think about it, there wouldn't be a show without an audience. Hence, you have to love and appreciate them. Remind them all the time how special they are and they will appreciate you in return.

Most times, your spectators might not be interested in how difficult your life is off the stage. They may not care if you had a stressful day or if you are down. They still anticipate a perfect performance each time. So you need to meet up to their expectations regardless.

While performing, your audience should be the star and not you. Don't go on and on about how awesome your feats are. They will just get bored easily. No one likes an egocentric person especially if you are an artist.

## The Basics in Mentalism

Before you become a pro in mentalism, you must be grounded in the basics. Being grounded in the basics means the ability to do the following:

### Make quick and educated judgments

Being able to trust your judgment is one of the vital steps towards becoming a good mentalist. It is quite unfortunate that many people have neglected this part. Being able to make a general and covert examination of a person provides basic information that may have been missed initially.

For instance, a man has a pen mark on his left arm and his ring finger is slightly tanned. This could be an indication that he is right-handed, separated, or divorced. A lot of things that can be physically observed such as the color or texture of a person's hand or the way a person dresses tells a lot about them.

### Act naturally

Being a mentalist demands that you tap into your talent and not become someone else. Although it is acceptable to adopt other people's techniques and routines, it is not acceptable to lose yourself.

If you are putting on a show, try not to make it a dramatic scene by forcing yourself into someone else's shoes. You will be more convincing if you act naturally and genuinely. Be slightly amused and relaxed at all times. Don't give people the impression that you are under pressure when you play out your tricks.

## Search for physical cues in others

A mentalist's job includes bringing an event or information that has been relegated to unconsciousness back to consciousness. Simply put, a mentalist stirs memories and causes you to remember even when you have forgotten.

Remember that even if someone does not remember, the brain has a record of every information seen, heard, or felt. Therefore every information you need is in the brain even though it might not be available at a particular point in time.

To practice mentalism, you need to learn to make inferences from physical cues presented by an audience. Such physical cues could include constriction and dilation of the pupil, heart rate, breathing rate, and relative perspiration.

## Use yourself as your first guinea pig

Although different people have their distinctive features, most behaviors in human beings are consistent. Your job will be made a whole lot easier if you know what it is you are looking for in a person. Start by studying yourself. Get in front of a mirror for more effective results.

Normally positive memories cause a dilation of the pupils while negative memories cause a constriction of the pupils. Think of how certain answers to certain questions will make you react. For instance, when you ask yourself what you love most about the beach, you are likely to visualize it first even before saying it.

If your answer was fire, you probably looked up while you visualized it. If your answer was the sound and smells on the beach, your eyes likely remained at eye level. If however, you thought of sand, your next gesture would be to look down. Generally, visual memories go up. aural memories remain on the level and hands-on memories compel one to gaze downwards.

## Memorize a "baseline" of behavior for your audience

This is a gentle reminder that certain situations cause some people to react in certain ways. People are different and reading them would be easier if you memorize a baseline of their behaviors. That way you will know how receptive your audience will be.

For instance, people who flirt naturally tend to become touchy when they are comfortable. They laugh out loud and tease people they find attractive.

On the other hand, some other people might not tolerate this behavior even when they are comfortable. Different people have different ways of expressing the same type of emotion. As a mentalist, you should know this much.

## Detect false information

If you can detect lies, you are one step to knowing what your audience is thinking. The measure of a person's pulse, blood pressure, and perspiration rate can tell if a person is lying or not. A person is more likely to be lying if these numbers are high.

When someone avoids eye contact with you or fiddles with their thumb, it could be an indication that the person is lying. Inconsistency in verbal and non-verbal expressions can also mean dishonesty.

## Listen actively

In reality, people tell us more than we hear. If you listen better, you will be amazed at the wealth of information you will gather. Learning to listen actively takes practice. But when you finally learn, your brain will be modified to make connections and you will be able to see the not-so-obvious things. This is one big secret in mentalism.

As a mentalist, you should be able to read in between the lines. Understand what your audience really means even when they don't say it out loud. For instance, if a friend approaches you and says "Oh Lord! I have been working out so hard". What this friend means to say is "Please,

I need to be told that I am fit and encouraged". This underlying clue is the doorway to a person's thoughts.

## Detect and interpret micro-expressions

To become a good mentalist, you need to master the art of detecting micro-expressions. These include the smallest little details that express the true feeling of a person before the conscious cover-up begins to set in. These micro-expressions are often little flashes of negative feelings or distress, most of which they don't want anyone to see.

You can detect a lie by paying close attention to your audience's entire body movements. How much they gulp, how they stand in relation to you or what they do with their hands. If someone is standing at an angle towards the door while you converse, it could be an indication that this person is trying to escape subconsciously. People tend to do this when they lie or keep secrets.

# Advanced Methods to Improve Your Mentalism If You Want To Be a Pro

## Mentalist's Choice

This technique is used in mentalism. It is used to get a person to freely make a choice when in an actual sense, you are choosing exactly what the mentalist wants you to choose.

For instance, a mentalist tells you to choose between two books. If you choose book 1 which the mentalist has initially prepared for the performance, he will go ahead. However, if you choose book 2, the mentalist will simply say "ok, we get rid of that one".

At the end of the day, the mentalist ends up using the same book he planned to use regardless of what your choice is. There are much more variations for this trick. Some are more complicated than others but one thing they have in common is that when used on a spectator, the person ends up falling right where the mentalist wants him or her to fall.

## Barnum Statements

Remember, I said we would get back to this topic in earlier chapters? Well, here we are! This entails using statements that are specially structured to appear specific and personal to a particular person. However, these statements seem to be true to most people.

Sometimes you believe a certain statement is specific to you not because of the way Barnum statements are designed. You may choose to believe a statement because inside of you, you want that statement to be true even though it is not. Unconsciously, such people gradually talk themselves into believing it. For instance, if a mentalist says "I think you are a kind of person who is introverted sometimes but when you decide to mingle, you give it your all". All this statement implies is that you are alone sometimes and you socialize sometimes. This statement, although it sounds specific, applies to most people but at that time, you are not going to recognize it.

Barnum statements are mostly used in horoscopes. Every time, readers want to believe in their horoscope more than they think. So when the horoscope throws a statement at them, they regard it as specific and convince themselves that the information is correct. Another name for Barnum statements is Forer effects and rainbow rouses.

## Blindfold Routines

Since the concepts of mentalism came to be, many types of blindfold routines have been carried out by various mentalists. This routine is considered dangerous. Most times, it ranges from Russian roulette to walking barefooted over sharp edge objects. One of the latest forms of blindfold routine is driving while blindfolded.

During this performance, the spectator normally sits on the passenger's seat. From there, he watches the mentalist drive as fast as possible while avoiding many obstacles on his way. There are few ways to perform this trick. The first is by using cheap blindfolds that allow the mentalist to see through. This method is least effective and is rarely used because any spectator can find this out easily.

The second is by employing muscular memory. In this method, the blindfolds used are not cheap ones and the mentalist can't see through them. But the trick here is that the mentalist must have spent many weeks learning how to drive that same distance at that particular location, over and over again. With enough practice, carrying out this routine will seem almost natural. One important thing the mentalist needs to get is a good cameraman and a spectator who will give away the right reaction.

The most modern way of performing the blindfold routine is by using an inconspicuous GPS. This GPS will communicate the directions to the mentalist via a hidden earpiece. The GPS will give the directions so the driver will know when to turn left or when to turn right. This performance can even be made easier using cruise control.

## Spikes and Cups

Spikes and cups is another method in mentalism that is being used over and over again but each time with slight modifications. This trick involves a base with a very sharp nail or blade. Sometimes, there could be bases without nails or sharp blades. Four or more disposable cups are assembled. These cups should be big enough to completely cover the dangerous base (nails or blades).

The performer will now instruct the spectator to cover the base that contains the nail and mix it up with the others. After the spectator does this, the mentalist will begin smashing the cups with his bare hands until he gets to the last one that contains the sharp object.

A dramatic "fake-out" is used at the end to make it look las if the mentalist is about to crush the wrong cup but of course, he won't. The mentalist might just claim he was able to identify the cups because he could read the spectator's eye movement and body language. This is just a simple trick, different mentalists have different ways of identifying which cup is the dangerous one.

One way of differentiating the dangerous cup from the rest is by using the cups number. Different cups will have different numbers but most times, the spectator doesn't notice because they are so engrossed in the process. However, these numbers are very visible to the mentalist because he is very much aware of them. If the trick is going to be done this way, then the performer will place the cup over the nail himself. That way he will be able to see which cup has the nail under it. He either turns around or is blindfolded while the spectator shifts the cups around.

Note: This trick can go wrong if the spectator removes the cup covering the nail and switches it with another cup. At this point, the trick becomes quite dangerous even though the performer is a pro.

The second way of performing this trick is by using the number of bases that go under the cups. Not just the number of one cup. While the other cups have normal bases, only one cup will have a different base (the dangerous one). A small length of fishing line is carefully attached to the dangerous cup. This fishing line is usually visible to the mentalist who knows it is there but the spectator cannot see it.

The advantage of this method is that the fishing line is always attached to the cup with a dangerous base. So no matter how much the spectator moves the cup, the performer will still be able to identify the cup. This method is relatively safer than the previous method described above. No matter the numbers written on the cup, the fishing line will help the performer identify the dangerous cup each time, every time. The only time this trick can go bad is when the fishing line falls off or if another thread is mistaken from the fishing line.

## Conclusion

As it has been mentioned earlier, learning to become a pro in mentalism is a gradual process. Mentalism itself is an art of patience and tactics. It demands talent, courage, dedication, and hard work. Although the whole process can be very difficult, it is not impossible provided you tap into the right resources and show willingness to learn. We are almost at the end of this incredible journey. To wrap things up, let's take a look at the concluding chapter and summary.

# Conclusion

———

You have to admit that we have had a wonderful ride throughout this book. The aim of this book was to teach you how to read people and know their secret desires.

I believe that you have got the complete gist and methods on how to make this possible.

This chapter is the concluding chapter and the summary of everything that this book has said so far.

So, we will take a quick look at the summary according to the chronological chapters of this book.

## What this book has delivered

### 1. Understanding Mentalism

In chapter one, we talked about the origin of mentalism. This book discussed the various stages of psychology until mentalism was formed. That's not all we did!

We also discussed mentalism and how it related to hypnosis, psychics, and telepathy. We also looked at the ties between mentalism and psychology. If you remember correctly, these ties are rock solid. If you don't remember that chapter yet, you should go back and read it again.

We also talked about how you can become a mentalist if you truly want and the qualities you might cultivate. Right now, we know how important qualities such as observation skills can change your chances in being a successful mentalist. After reading this book, you should be confident that you can make that happen.

## 2. The Importance of Mentalism

In chapter two, we talked more about the importance of mentalism. At the end of this book, you have to agree with me that the importance is just immeasurable.

Mentalism allows you to do things that others would dream of. From understanding people's emotions to working in various industries, you have a real gem if you master the mentalist tricks. We also talked about the various things you should probably know before you go full-time in mentalism.

## 3. The Art of Cold Reading

Personally, the art of cold reading has always been my best part of mentalism. In chapter three, we discussed all of it. As you probably noticed, cold reading kept on coming up throughout the book.

One prominent part of cold reading is Barnum's statements. If you haven't already started practicing your statements, you should start already.

We also talked about other practices. One of the easiest techniques to start with will be shotgunning. It's easy once you have a basic idea of what's needed.

In this chapter, we also discussed how practice can quicken the learning process of cold reading.

## 4. Body Languages

Chapters four and five are arguably the chapters with the juiciest information. Delving deep into reading someone's body language. In fact, those two chapters are the main ingredients you need if you want to know what people want or desire.

In this chapter, we focus mostly on human gestures, emotions, and motivations. However, motivations were treated as a separate topic in chapter 7.

We also talked about why body languages are important to mentalists. One of the biggest reason why mentalists have to know what body languages mean is that it allows them to build close ties with the participant.

You should grasp properly what was discussed in this chapter. It is crucial if you want to become a mentalist.


## 5. Reading People's Intentions

People's intentions can be hard to spot. This is true as many learn over time to mask their true intentions behind bland faces.

This chapter discusses the many ways in which a mentalist can read the intentions of people. Some of these intentions include how to spot a liar. We even talked a bit about courtship signals and how you can easily see who is attracted to who in a room.

It's a fantastic chapter. If you skipped it, you should probably go back and read it.


## 6. Personality Differences and Mentalism

We talked about various personality differences and why mentalists have to know more about these differences. The reactions that you will get from an extrovert for example will be totally different from those of an introvert.

Understanding this is one of the ways to avoid making mistakes in your readings. Some things that apply to an extrovert will simply not apply to an introvert and vice versa. That's just the way it is!

## 7. Motivations Are Huge For Mentalists

If you want to become a mentalist, then you have to learn how to read people's motivations. They are very important. There are so many categories of motivations.

So, if you skip this chapter, you should probably go back and read it. We also talked about how mentalists can use motivation to quickly analyze and assess a situation. That chapter is a true lifesaver!

## 8. Mentalist Tricks Galore

In chapter 8 of this book, we went on a journey to learning about the various gestures and tricks a mentalist can use.

This chapter includes every little trick you can think of. It is really the ideal way to learn about all the tricks a mentalist should have under his sleeves. If you are fortunate enough, you should understand most parts of this chapter in one go.

If you missed this, please go back and read this chapter completely.

## 9. Keep On Improving

The last chapter focuses on how you can keep on improving your mentalist tricks. Again, we talked about how the effective use of Barnum statements can be the key to getting a head start as a mentalist. It can also help you understand what other people really want in life.

When you combine these chapters, what you get is a complete guide on everything you need to understand in people's behaviors, motivations, emotions, and even gestures. Most of all, it leaves with you a guide on how to become a mentalist.

Before I leave for good, here are some of the best tips moving forward:

# What You Should Do After Reading This Book

## 1. Don't Rest On Your Laurels

It's tempting to close this book, give a huge sigh and go back to business as usual. However, if you want to be a mentalist, you have to start working on it right now.

I'd like to think that you were already practicing as you were reading this book. If you were not, then you should probably start now. There are a lot of dangers if you do not start now. First, you will probably forget most of the things you have read and have to go through all the tips again. That's a long journey that might be very discouraging.

You could also simply lose interest in the whole journey. So, if this is really what you want to do, don't let that happen!

## 2. Do More Research

While this book gives you a good head start, you must keep on researching about mentalists and their various skills. Fortunately for us, we live in a world that has immediate access to a lot of resources. So, videos, books, and courses are all at your disposal.

All you really have to do is to pick what you want to learn. Of course, you can always return to this book to relearn some of the useful methods outlined here.

## 3. Join a Community

Just like any other profession or discipline, you are not the only one. There is a large number of mentalists from around the world. There are several reasons why you just have to connect with them.

First, they have been in this business way longer than you have. Therefore, they will know a lot of things that you probably never knew. They will also know how to monetize your skills in the best possible way.

So, you won't just be a mentalist because that is what you love. You'll also be able to make some money for all your troubles.

So, do some research about some good mentalist communities you can join. Then, once you are sure this is the right fit for you, do not hesitate to take the leap.

It might not work out...

Despite your best efforts, it might not work out. You should know that it is perfectly normal. Some people are talented but not just for mentalism.

Sometimes, you might not be ready for the commitment it requires. If that is the case for you, then you should probably try again when you are ready.

Mentalism has been around for a long time now. It will definitely still be around when you are ready.

## 4. Finally, Practice

In anything that you do, practice and consistency are vital. You have to be consistent as the good things usually don't come in just a day. It's through consistent practice that you will be able to understand many things needed to be a mentalist.

Also, try to improve your observation skills. You'll be surprised at what you'll be able to achieve!

So, what if you could know what people are thinking? Yes, you can and it's not magic! It's simply mentalism!.

Printed by Amazon.

Financementor
16 rue du Pont Neuf, 75001 Paris, France

Printed in Great Britain
by Amazon

42095009R00086